CW00350382

Black Belt Thinking

59 strategies for success in life and business

Nick Forgham

Fisher King Publishing

Black Belt Thinking

Copyright © Nick Forgham 2016

ISBN 978-1-910406-42-7

All rights reserved. No part of this publication may be reproduced or distributed in any form or by any means, or stored in a data-base or retrieval system, without the prior written permission of Fisher King Publishing.

Cover design by Charlotte O'Neil
Main image by Romanova Natali

Fisher King Publishing Ltd
The Studio, Arthington Lane
Pool-in-Wharfedale
LS21 1JZ
England
www.fisherkingpublishing.co.uk

To Lynne

Thank you for the journey we have shared.
Here's to the journey ahead of us.

To Juliette, Jacqueline, Jack and Lauren.

Four exceptional young people on amazing
journeys and it is a privilege to be part of them.

Foreword

The concepts and strategies described in this book are the very concepts and strategies that are behind BNI's success.

BNI started just over 30 years ago, with a meeting I held at my house. It is now an international organisation that is active in more than 65 countries, has nearly 200,000 members, and generated $9.3 billion (USD) of business for its members in 2015 alone.

The process I have personally been through as a business owner mirrors the sections of this book.

From that first meeting in my house I developed Awareness. Awareness of the power of referrals and recommendations, and Awareness that there was a major gap in the market. People just love referrals!

I developed Strategies to make the meetings effective, where we started to generate a lot of business for each other. And then Strategies to grow the business.

There were times when things did not go according to plan. During these times I needed to keep my Spirit high. And not just my own Spirit. Just as Nick covers in the book, there were beliefs that I became Aware of, Beliefs that were limiting the growth of the business. By overcoming these Beliefs I and my growing team were able to accelerate the growth of the business. The power of Humility was a key factor in BNI becoming successful internationally. By looking at the bigger picture, being Aware of the needs of other people and how we could help them be successful played a major part in developing our team internationally. By keeping it simple, we made the language of referrals and BNI an international success.

There were many times when we could have got caught up in planning, in waiting for the perfect moment. But as a Black belt in Karate I know that sometimes you just have to go! So we would just make a Decision to go, to do it now, and learn from any mistakes.

These concepts are vital to the success of ANY business. And they can be applied to our personal lives too.

You don't have to be a Black belt in karate to understand these concepts. You don't have to be a Black belt to be able to implement them effectively in your personal life or in your business life.

These concepts and strategies are available to everyone.

This book shows you how to get them and how to use them.

I hope you enjoy this book.

Ivan Misner
Founder & Chief Visionary Officer of BNI
Black Belt in Karate

Introduction

One day a high-ranking Japanese Black Belt, a master and *sensei* (teacher) many times over, met up with a friend, an old man who he knew from long ago. Throughout the conversation, the karate Black Belt master continually referred to the old man as '*sensei*'.

But the old man was not a master of a martial art. The old man was not a Black Belt. In fact, he had never studied a martial art.

The reason the Black Belt master called the old man '*sensei*' was because he WAS a *sensei*. A *sensei* of life.

We are all *senseis*. *Senseis* of our own life. We are on a journey to be a master, a master of ourselves.

Black Belts do not have any special magical powers. Let's dispel that myth right now!

What they do have is a mindset and an approach to life that generally serves them well. My aim in writing this book is to share this mindset with you, for you to select any parts that can be of help to you on your journey.

How to get the most from this book

You can read this book chronologically, or you can dip in and out.

Each chapter has one thing that you can do there and then. You may like to stop and think about a chapter when you have just finished reading it, or move on to the next one straight away.

The premise behind this book

Karate is the metaphor used in this book to explain a concept or idea. By viewing things from a different perspective we can gain insight into a particular issue or challenge. Viewing it differently means we engage the vast resources of our brain in a different way, shedding light on a particular challenge, or enabling us to spot a new opportunity.

Throughout the book, some of the concepts and strategies covered are applied to networking. They can equally be applied to any area that is of relevance to you, in your personal life or in your business life. It just happens that networking is something that I know something about.

How the book is structured

Chapters 1-50 take us to Black belt. Chapters 51-59 take us beyond Black Belt, because Black Belt is only the beginning.

The first three chapters introduce some of the key concepts we will be covering. From Chapter Four onwards we look at specific techniques, strategies and concepts that we can apply to our personal and business lives.

Please note that the information contained in this book does not constitute medical advice. There are some things that I do for my health and well-being, which I believe serve me well, but that does not mean they are good for you. Do not try these at home (or anywhere else).

All views expressed are those of the author.

Nick Forgham

"Darkness cannot drive out darkness;
only light can do that.
Hate cannot drive out hate;
only love can do that."

Martin Luther King, Jr.
Humanitarian and civil rights activist

Contents

Section 3 Spirit

Section 4 Humility

Section 5 Decision

Part Two   Black Belt To Master

Part One
Black Belt Thinking

Awareness

1. Zanshin

When I teach self-defence courses, I stress that the most important thing we will cover is *zanshin*.

Zanshin means awareness. It literally means remaining mind. It is the relaxed alertness that we have after having done a karate technique. It is also the continual state of alertness of mind we have in our daily lives before, during and after any event.

Everything starts with *zanshin*. Until we are aware of something, we cannot respond to it. If we do something exceptional, unless we are aware of what we have done, we cannot consciously recreate it.

If we make a mistake and are not aware we have made a mistake, we have no opportunity to learn from it. So there is a good chance we will make the same mistake, or one similar, again.

In sales, the classic example of low *zanshin*, where we drop our guard, is buyer's remorse. We think we have got the order, but there is something else that we are not AWARE of. And the prospect doesn't buy anything from us, or buys from someone else.

Zanshin and success

In business, people and companies that have the most *zanshin* are the most successful. They respond quicker to outside dangers and opportunities, because they see things before others do.

They are more tuned in to their environment, to what is going on around them.

Most Black Belts that I know have never used their karate in a self-defence situation. The main reason for this is that they have a finely developed sense of *zanshin*. They have spotted the danger before it becomes critical, and adapted accordingly.

> When my children were very young, my wife and I went to visit her parents just outside Bournemouth, on the south coast. We took the opportunity of some free babysitting for just the two of us to go to a pub in Poole, a few miles along the coast. Not much happens in Poole. The local joke is that people retire and move to Bournemouth, and when they die they go to Poole.
>
> We were in a quiet pub, in the early evening, having a drink. After a while, I noticed a group of three men, standing at the bar, looking at me. And not in a particularly friendly way.
>
> They didn't fit in with the other people in the pub. They seemed nervous, agitated, excited, like something had just happened or was about to.
>
> I noticed that they carried on looking over in my direction. My wife said they were also looking at her! And had been since they came in the pub.
>
> I had just got my first Dan, so was a Black Belt in karate.
>
> All the signs were that they were looking for a fight. It was time for action!
>
> I stood up, got my coat, and with me in-between my wife and the men at the bar we walked out of the pub, got in the car and drove back to her parents.

And that's the end of the story. I have never been attacked, and hopefully never will be.

We can do this in our lives and in our business. We can be one step ahead of the game, avoiding trouble and conflict. We will spot dangers and threats before they become critical, whether in a relationship, in a physical setting, or in our business lives.

In business we can avoid the fights and battles that our competitors will become embroiled in and instead focus on our business and our plans. This means we will be more alert to opportunities and new situations that we can take advantage of.

Be first to react

With more *zanshin* we have more agility and adaptability.

We can only react to the things that we are aware of. So the more aware we are, the quicker we will react.

This book is essentially about *zanshin*. That state where we are at one with our environment, feeling tuned in. Moving as part of something bigger than ourselves, aiming to create good in the world, for ourselves and others. It is about how we get there and what it feels like when we have.

In self-defence, the concept of *zanshin* can save your life. Having a highly developed sense of *zanshin* is not just the same as knowing a number of self-defence techniques. Having high *zanshin* takes you ABOVE the level of technique, which is what this books aims to do.

This book is about the mindset of a Black Belt, and how we can apply this mindset to all aspects of our lives.

Black Belts know that by having more *zanshin* (awareness) we will be quicker to evade dangers, and quicker to spot opportunities.

One Thing You Can DO Now:

Start to expand and develop your awareness. Think of something that has worked well for you recently, perhaps in your business life or your personal life. Can you identify one thing that made this turn out well for you?

2. Self And Responsibility

The first thing to be aware of, is us. Who ARE we?
The first step in being able to control our self, is to be aware of our self.
To know who we are. The awareness comes first. Our self is a mixture of
many things. We are a combination of our strengths (and weaknesses), our
beliefs, our fears, our systems and processes, the programs that we run,
our ego, our values, the journey that we are on and many other things. All
these and more are covered in this book.

Know yourself
Awareness of self, of us, is a key concept in philosophy, traditional martial
arts and modern life.

"Know yourself and know others, and in
1,000 battles you will never be in peril."
Gichin Funakoshi, the 'father of modern day karate'

The first two words are the key. Know yourself. Being aware of who WE are
is fundamental to OUR success, in life and in business.

One who knows others is wise
One who knows himself is wisest
One who conquers others is strong
One who conquers himself is strongest
Lao-Tzu (Ancient Chinese philosopher and writer, founder of Taoism)

When we know ourselves, then we can take responsibility for our self. From
there we can focus on things outside of 'us', and have an impact on things
outside of our self.
Taking responsibility is the first of Jack Canfield's *Success Principles (Take*
100% Responsibility For Your Life). The first three of Stephen Covey's *7*
Habits of Highly Effective People all deal with mastery of the self.

Self is all we have. The Japanese word '*Kara*' means empty, and '*te*'
means hand. '*Kara te*' thus means empty hand. It means that all we have

got is us, our self. It also means that all we need, is our self.

> One of my karate students was a child actor who had parts in some of the Harry Potter films. He had been training for four years, and at 16 years old was six weeks from his first Dan (Black Belt) grading. Although his actual techniques were good, he was destined to fail.
>
> At the end of a Black Belt grading there is one minute of pure free fighting. No pads or mitts, just a gum shield because of a nasty accident in a previous Black Belt grading where someone nearly lost all their front teeth. As well as good techniques, we have to show spirit. And his problem was that during the fighting his posture was poor, meaning that his techniques were slow and weak, and he could not show martial spirit. Whatever we worked on to get his posture upright did not work. As soon as he came to fight, his posture changed.
>
> In a one hour grading exam, everything can be lost in that last 60 seconds. Black Belts have to show that they CAN fight.
>
> I had tried everything to get his posture upright, rather than crouched and defensive, where he was protecting his stomach but making his techniques weak and lacking spirit.
>
> The one thing that changed him, in a moment, was when I shouted "IT IS NOT WHAT THEY WILL DO TO YOU BUT WHAT YOU CAN DO TO THEM."
>
> That was the trigger. He became upright, his techniques were sharper, he could move better, and show good spirit.
>
> And he passed his grading. First time.

Internalise or externalise

This concept is known as Locus of Control. It is the difference between what we internalise and what we externalise. When we have a high Locus of Control, we internalise things, we take ownership of them, we take responsibility. When we have a low Locus of Control we externalise them, we pass control over to someone else.

My karate student had been externalising, focusing on the attacks, whatever they may be, whenever they may occur. When he internalised, and focused on what HE could do, he had confidence. He had a Black Belt posture and a Black Belt spirit.

It was by internalising that he was able to fight off the external attacks!

In business we have to internalise to know who we are. To know ourselves and know our business. To have awareness of our internal strengths and weaknesses, so that we can match these to external threats and opportunities.

Successful business people know themselves, and take responsibility for themselves.

> *"In traditional karate-do we always keep in mind*
> *that the true opponent is oneself."*
> Gichin Funakoshi

Black Belts are aware of what we have internalised, of the things that makes us who we are, which is the first step to developing our self.

One Thing You Can DO Now:

Think about an idea, or concept, or belief that you have recently taken on-board. Be aware that this is something you have internalised, that has become part of you.

3. Being Present

The way to increase our *zanshin*, to feel more connected, is to be present. This applies to our personal lives and to our business.

When we are present, we are living in the now. We are engaged with our senses. Noticing everything that goes on around us.

Mindfulness

Mindfulness is essentially a moving *zanshin*, where we are present and feel connected to what is around us.

In karate I first became aware of this concept during semi-free sparring. Here, your partner attacks you but first lets you know the attack he or she is about to launch. Then they pause, so that we are practicing for real.

Between the time when they announce their attack and when they actually start to move, at fast speed, believe me you are totally present! If you blink, they will immediately attack. If you relax too much, they will immediately attack. If you glance down or away, they will immediately attack.

In that moment of time, you are on full alert. You are aware of you, of them, of the floor, of everything. You have total *zanshin*. You are present, you are living in the now.

Are there times in your life when you feel totally present, focusing on the here and now? What are these times, and how do they make you feel connected to what is going on around you?

Being present and negative emotions

Many negative emotions and feelings are either memories of the past or worries about the future.

If we were to have guilt about something, it is unlikely we would feel guilty about something that may happen in the future. Guilt is a powerful emotion that is connected to the past.

Similarly, regret is an emotion that is concerned with the past. We tend to have regrets about things that have already happened, even though we know we can't change them.

There are also powerful negative emotions that are more concerned about the future. Two main ones are fear and anxiety. Generally, we are not fearful or anxious about something that has already happened. There may be consequences about something that has already happened, but the consequences are in the future.

Negative emotions sap our energy, making us feel tired and lethargic. They take up space in our head, meaning that we are not as focused and as in-tune with our environment and the people around us. When we live in the present, to a large extent we are free of some powerful negative emotions. By itself, this frees our minds of clutter and negativity. Living in the present enables us to develop our *zanshin* and become aware of things that do matter, things over which we have some control.

PAST : FUTURE
Guilt : Fear
Regret : Anxiety

Focusing on being present, connected to what is happening right now, will improve our *zanshin*. And when we are present we feel more connected on a larger scale. In our business lives this could mean that we are better able to see the implications of new regulations or laws. Better tuned in to emerging markets and new large-scale opportunities.

Black Belts know that being present will give us zanshin, where we are more connected to what is around us, in life and in business.

One Thing You Can DO Now:

Focus on you in the present, in the here and now. Keep focusing on the present, and ask yourself what you are anxious or afraid of that is happening NOW. The chances are that there will not be anything to be anxious or afraid of right now. Ask yourself how this feels.

4. Mokuso (time out)

Mokuso is how we become more in the present.
Mokuso increases our awareness.

> On 2nd August 2014 I was admitted as an emergency case to my local hospital. I had a severe urinary tract infection, and was screaming in pain. None of the four different types of oral pain killers that I was given, including morphine, had any effect. I was hooked up to heart monitors, and one of my thoughts was that I would die, or pass out, or have a heart attack (in which case I would die or pass out).
> It was only when I was hooked up intravenously, after five hours of screaming and intense pain, that the pain started to disappear.
> The following morning I woke up pain free, in the hospital, and realised my heart was beating way too fast.
> But I didn't want any more drugs, any more tests, any more fuss.
> So I did *Mokuso*.
> And in two minutes my heart was normal, and continued to beat at a normal rate.

Mokuso is a simple breathing technique.

Aligning the conscious and unconscious

When we focus on our breathing, we are aligning our conscious mind with our unconscious mind.

Our conscious mind is where we consciously think, where we process inputs from our five senses. Our unconscious mind is pretty much everything else. It includes our autonomic nervous system, which is the part of our body that does little things like keep us alive, like tell our heart to carry on beating! Our unconscious mind is about our very survival. For example, it is impossible to voluntarily asphyxiate yourself (do NOT try this at home, just accept it as fact!).

Some estimates say that our conscious mind is 2% of what we have mentally at our disposal, and our unconscious mind is the other 98%.

When we focus on our breathing, we are accessing the power of our unconscious mind, because we are aligning the two minds. We are also aligning our mind AND our body.

So by relaxing, by taking time out, we become massively more powerful.

"To the mind that is still, the whole universe surrenders."
Lao-Tzu

Doing Mokuso

The Karate *Mokuso* meditation technique is very simple and, as I found out in hospital, very effective.

Get yourself comfortable, somewhere you can relax.

Breathe in through your nose, and imagine the air you have breathed in as a solid object, about the size of your thumb, about 8cm long and about 2cm wide.

As you breathe in the thumb (breath) goes up your nose, up your forehead and down the back of your head. It then goes down the spine, and tucks under the bottom of the torso and comes up into your stomach. It then goes up through your chest, and out through your mouth.

This whole process takes about 10 seconds.

Then breathe in and start again.

All the time focus on the breath and how it travels up over, down and up through the body.

The out-breath is just as important as the in-breath, if not more so.

The technique works best if you close your eyes, so that you are free to focus purely on the breath.

Taking some time out, even if just for two minutes, can give us time to refresh, to relax, to put things in perspective.

Be connected in business

Now imagine your business where you feel totally aligned on your goals, and have full awareness and understanding of your environment. You are CONNECTED!

The conscious part of your business is the day to day activities that you are aware of as you are doing them. Sure, they are important, but probably not always critical. (If you go on holiday the business will still operate.)

The unconscious part of your business are the elements that you are not aware of on a day to day basis. Lead generation activities; the goodwill amongst your customers; the strength of your personal and business brand in your respective markets; money received into the business; your accounts; and more. If these elements disappear, so does the business. Doing some business *Mokuso* will align these two powerful forces, and increase our *zanshin*.

Take time out

Get some *Mokuso* in to your life by taking time out. Pause and reflect before looking at your computer or phone. Occasionally turn your chair and face away from your monitor, and do nothing. Go for a walk and leave your phone on your desk. Go and play golf. Go and sit somewhere.

Black Belts know that we can burn ourselves out. If we are too intense, always focused on doing, doing, doing, it is not sustainable. Life, and business, is a marathon not a sprint.

And we miss opportunities, and fail to spot danger, because our *zanshin* is low. So we are not as effective or as efficient as we could be.

We are human beings, not human doings.

Black Belts take time out, perhaps for just two minutes at a time, to align all our forces and increase our zanshin so that we can move and react quicker.

One Thing You Can DO Now:

If you are listening to this book while driving or doing some other activity that requires your full attention, carry on doing what you are doing and ignore the next 10 seconds.

Assuming you are READING this book, before turning this page, close your eyes, assuming it is safe to do so, and do some Mokuso. 10 nice, deep breaths, that will take about two minutes, will clear your mind and increase your zanshin.

5 Values

Values are judgments about how important something is to us. We may be aware of our values consciously, or we may not.

Our values are unique to us and are a key part of who we are. By knowing and understanding our values, we become more aware of who we are.

Motivation

Values, along with other things, drive our behaviour and our actions, which drives our results.

Our motivation comes from our values system.

In karate, the values of this traditional martial art are clearly stated in what is known as the *Dojo Kun* (which literally translates as Training Hall Rules). The *Dojo Kun* constitutes the underlying principles of karate.

In classes I have attended where we have recited the *Dojo Kun*, it is always stated with sincerity. We say it because we mean it.

DOJO KUN

Hitotsu! Jinkaku kansei ni tsutomuru koto!
One! To strive for the perfection of character!

Hitotsu! Makoto no michi o mamoru koto!
One! To defend the paths of truth!

Hitotsu! Doryoku no seishin o yashinau koto!
One! To foster the spirit of effort!

Hitotsu! Reigi o omonsuru koto!
One! To honour the principles of etiquette!

Hitotsu! Kekki no yu o imashimuru koto!
One! To guard against impetuous courage!

Summarising, it is about perfecting character, truth, effort, etiquette and not being rash.

Having these clearly stated means that the whole ethos behind what we do is understood. This is important because sometimes we need to go on a bit of a journey to find out what is important to us.

Finding our values

What is important to you?

Maybe it is family. Maybe you have a hard work ethic, in always committing fully to things. Maybe you value honesty, and fair play. Other values such as caring, forgiveness, generosity, courage, reliability or excellence are all examples of personal values.

Successful businesses also have clear values. They know what is important to them. And it is the values of the company that give the business its culture.

When I teach self-defence courses, the second most important thing I teach (after *Zanshin*), is that if someone in a threatening or potentially threatening situation asks for your phone, wallet or handbag, just give it to them. When we get stressed, our values get discombobulated, and we can temporarily value a bit of plastic or a small amount of money over our health and well-being.

Black Belts know what is important, and what isn't. Black Belts know their values, the code by which they live their lives.

This makes saying Yes or No to various opportunities more straight-forward. If something is in line with our values, we can consider it. If it isn't, we don't.

Black Belts know that being aware of our values gives us a greater awareness of our self, so that we can understand our behaviour and our actions.

One Thing You Can DO Now:

Take some time out, perhaps using Mokuso, and reflect on the things that are important to you.

6 What We Do Know

Black Belts are aware of what they do know, and what they don't.
And quite often, when we think about it, we actually know far more than we at first think we do!
In karate we have *katas*. A *kata* is a sequence of moves, which in some other traditional martial arts are called patterns. Each *kata* consists of 20-65 movements. And there are 27 karate *kata*!
This adds up to more than 900 moves, with each move being a different technique in a different stance, usually in a different direction. That's a lot to remember.
There are very few people who could just do all 27 *kata* in one go. But there are many more people who could probably work out each *kata* after a few goes. They DO know it, it is just not quite to hand.

We know so much

And this is the same basis by which we live many aspects of our lives.
We DO know what to do, we DO understand what is going on. When we stop to think about it, we know far more than we think we do.

> One of the greatest ever UK karate competitors was *Sensei* Terry O'Neill. He was teaching a course I attended, and told the story of how, when he passed his Third Dan Black Belt, he went to his instructor and asked to be shown a new technique.
> His instructor replied that were no more techniques. There are only so many techniques, and as a Third Dan Black Belt he knew them all! He was advised to continue training hard, put on some weight to build power but to keep his speed and agility. And that is what he did.
> He had reached the level where there were no more techniques. He knew everything he needed to know. Terry O'Neill went on to captain the British Squad that won the 1975 World Championships in Los Angeles.

Focus on knowing and stop searching

This is a bit like life. We can waste a lot of time searching for the next thing, feeling incomplete without 'it'. But we don't know what 'it' is!

The chances are we already have it. Sure, there are new things we could learn; new perspectives that we could adopt that might give us a crucial insight into some problem. But we pretty much know all we need to know. Being AWARE of what we know is the main thing. It is more important to know what we know, than to search for some miracle.

By focusing on *zanshin*, we can become aware of all the things that we do know.

Having awareness of what we do know is the mindset of a Black Belt.

From knowledge, the stuff we already do know, comes wisdom.

> Knowledge is knowing a tomato is a fruit
> Wisdom is not putting it in a fruit salad.

Black Belts are aware of what they do know.

One Thing You Can DO Now:

Think about your life so far and everything you have done, have been taught, have ever accomplished. These are all things that you already know.

7 Circle Of Life

The concept of Internalising and Externalising discussed in Chapter Two is a key concept to be aware of.

In martial arts the concept was best explained by Bruce Lee. Standing upright, he stuck one leg out behind him, gently touching the floor. He then rotated his body a full 360 degrees, making a circle around his body at the point where this leg touched the floor.

Kiss or kill

This is your Circle of Life. From a self-defence perspective, you want to know who is inside your circle! The people inside your circle will either kiss you, or kill you.

Do not take this literally! Especially at parties or networking events. Just because someone is not about to plant a big kiss on you does NOT mean they are about to kill you! In other words, just because someone has not kissed you does not mean that they are about to attack you and that therefore it is OK to attack them.

Imagine that where you are sitting or standing (or even lying) right now there is your Circle of Life around you. This is YOUR circle, it is no-one else's. Even if there is someone sitting or standing (or lying) right next to you, within your circle, this is YOUR circle.

We control our circle

The key thing about the Circle of Life is that we can control what happens in our own circle. Not just people who are physically inside it, but everything that is within it. All our thoughts, our beliefs, our actions, our behaviour. The things inside our circle are things that we have let in to our circle, whether we are aware of them or not.

Empowerment

As we covered in Awareness 2 Self and Responsibility, having a high Locus of Control is where we internalise things. It is where we take full responsibility for what happens inside our Circle of Life.

Having a high Locus of Control, taking responsibility for our own circle, is empowering.

Consider the reactions below which follow on from having a high Locus of Control for when we succeed and fail, compared to a low Locus of Control:

Situation	Locus	Empowering?	Our reaction
When we succeed	High Locus	Yes	Give ourselves credit, reward ourselves. Are happier, more motivated.
	Low Locus	No	Believe it was down to luck, no increase in our self-esteem.
When we fail	High Locus	Yes	Take responsibility, learn from our mistakes. More likely to succeed next time.
	Low Locus	No	Refuse to take responsibility. Never develop, progress or learn.

So with a high Locus of Control, we tend to reward ourselves, learn from our mistakes and have more success.

With a low Locus of Control we maintain low self-esteem, and never develop or progress as we do not learn from our own mistakes.

Black Belts know that life is about them. It is about US. It is about taking responsibility for us, for what we have let in to our Circle, the things that will define who we are.

Karate Precept
"First control yourself before attempting to control others."

Take responsibility or be a victim

In some ways this is not an easy place to be. Taking responsibility for what happens in our life can be a massive step. An easy route is to put the blame on other factors, to just live as a victim, at the whim of circumstance and whatever happens to us next.

The Circle of Life can be likened to our Comfort Zone. Inside the zone is where we feel comfortable. It is outside the zone where we can feel uncomfortable. But it is outside our Comfort Zone where we learn.

Most beginners would not feel comfortable starting in a class where everyone else is a Black Belt.

But this is the best thing to do! They would learn faster, and more safely, and so progress quicker.

The bigger our zone, our circle, the more comfortable we feel. With a small Circle of Life, our Comfort Zone shrinks. There is just more stuff outside it! And we have less notice of things happening; we don't see them until they are in our face, which means we get hurt.

Expanding our Comfort Zone

The ultimate aim is to expand our Circle of Life as far as possible, so that we are comfortable. For some people this represents their life journey.

As we expand our Comfort Zone, the penultimate stage is to be comfortable being uncomfortable!

And the last stage, which we cover more in Humility, is where we feel connected to EVERYTHING, so we are comfortable everywhere. Because we are one part of the whole thing.

> *"Do not try to change the wind, change the sail."*
> From the Little Book of Seishinkai.

The thing about control is that although we only have SOME control over what happens to us (things outside our circle), we do have 100% control over how we react to it (which is inside our circle).

So we can take 100% responsibility for how we feel and react to things outside of our Circle.

Black Belts are aware of our Circle of Life, which we control and where we take responsibility for what happens inside it. Black Belts give themselves credit when they succeed, and take responsibility when they fail.

One Thing You Can DO Now:

Think of something good that happened to you recently. Which aspects of this can YOU take responsibility for? Give yourself credit, reward yourself.

8 Your Dojo Is Everywhere

The *Dojo* is the hall where we train in karate.
In Japanese, 'do' means way and 'jo' means place. Thus, *Dojo* means the place of the way. It is the place where we practice.

Karate precept
"Do not think that karate training is only in the dojo"

A karate saying is that all of life is a *Dojo*. Our *Dojo* is everywhere.

Being consistent, being us
This is about being consistent and congruent. It is about how, once we have used *Mokuso* and *Zanshin* to find ourselves, our values, we can be true to them all the time. Whatever situation or environment we find ourselves in.

The only way to find who we are, is to be who we are all the time. Not adopting roles that change from one minute to the next, so that we are not sure of who we are, or what role we are meant to adopt now.

The real me
Black Belts consistently present one face to the outside world, a face that represents the real 'me'. They have the courage that this 'face' may not be the most suitable for every situation, but nevertheless this 'face' is the real me.

> My instructor Malcolm Phipps had cancer several years ago. There was a period of time where it was a bit tricky, and he did not know if the prognosis was going to be a good one or a very serious one. Whenever I spoke with him on the phone during this period, he was the same person. Still laughing and joking, in a natural, unforced way. Still the same person. Still him.
> He made a full recovery.

When we know who we are, we are always in alignment, always true to our values and our true self. We are the same everywhere, to every person. This reduces stress and inner conflict in ourselves, as we do not have to

Awareness

focus energy on considering which role to adopt, which mannerisms to adopt. We can just be. We just are.

Constant awareness

This concept of everywhere being a *Dojo* also refers to our *zanshin* always being 'on'. Awareness is not something to turn off and on when we feel like it.

Opportunities, as well as dangers, present themselves at any time. With constant *zanshin* we will always be aware of dangers before they pose a major problem, or of opportunities before someone else spots them.

> *"Opportunities multiply as they are seized."*
> Sun Tzu (5th Century BC Chinese general and philosopher,
> author of *The Art Of War*)

In our modern society the biggest threat to *zanshin*, to being connected to what is around us, is focusing on mobile devices, or handhelds. These eat up our focus and attention. They are *zanshin* destroyers! They are training us to be not connected to what is around us, of other people, the immediate environment.

When we are not present we are not connected, meaning we have low *zanshin*. We are not training ourselves to develop our awareness.

Black Belts present one face, their true face, to themselves and to the outside world. They maintain their zanshin, because they know that trouble, and opportunities, occur when you least expect them.

One Thing You Can DO Now:

Be aware of things that may rob you of your zanshin, or where you feel obliged to take on a particular role that does not reflect your true self.

9 Risk

Having high *zanshin* will help to remove the risk in our daily lives. The risks to our personal safety in our personal lives, and the risks we face in our business lives.

Risk is defined as 'a situation involving exposure to danger.'

It is when we are not **AWARE** of the danger we have become exposed to, that a problem occurs.

The earlier we can be aware of the risk, the safer we will be. Whether in our personal lives or our businesses.

> I have been taught advanced self-defence against knife attacks. Facing a knife attack is very dangerous.
>
> The golden rule is that in most cases where a knife is used, the person receiving the attack never sees the knife!
>
> What saves them is their highly developed sense of *zanshin*.
>
> A nightclub security person I met had faced two knife attacks. One was from a man, one from a woman. In both cases he had not seen the knife. He had sensed they had a knife and had reacted accordingly, neutralising the attack. He was not harmed in either attack.

Risk and business

In business, it is important to be aware of the role of risk, and of how important risk is. Many successful companies have proven strategies to minimise risk:

Giving new employees a probation period is a strategy to reduce risk, for the employer.

Offering case studies and testimonials to prospective clients is a strategy to reduce risk.

Offering money-back guarantees to new and existing customers is a strategy to reduce risk.

Once we are aware of a specific risk, we can take action to minimise it.

Awareness

Risk and self-defence

Here is a question for the men:

> You are in an unsafe area and enter some public toilets. There is only one entrance. In front of you is a row of five urinals. Which one do you use? The one nearest to you, which is the one nearest the door? Or the one furthest away, where you would be able to see someone walking towards you? Or one of the ones in the middle?
>
> Got an answer?
>
> It is a trick question. In this type of environment, you use a cubicle. This minimises the risk.

Developing a state of high *zanshin* will remove most of the risks that we face.

Black Belts know that by continuing to develop their zanshin they will minimise the risks they face.

One Thing You Can DO Now:

Think of one risk facing you personally or in your business, and ask yourself what strategy you can adopt to minimise it.

10 Fun

Be aware that you need to have fun.

> *"In accordance with our principles of free enterprise and healthy competition, I'm going to ask you two to fight to the death for it."*
> Pantomime Horses, Monty Python

Life is about balance. Training in karate is hard. Life, sometimes, is hard. We need to balance this out with some humour and some fun.

Little old ladies

One of my previous instructors, a lovely man called Derek Barnet, used to tell us that it was very important to have *zanshin* of little old ladies. This is because little old ladies are very dangerous! Especially at bus stops.
Imagine the headline in the local newspaper if a karate Black Belt was somehow to get involved in a fight with a little old lady at a bus stop. And the little old lady won! The headline would be something like '93 Year Old Grandmother Beats Up Karate Expert.'We were warned that we would be described as an expert even if we had just completed our first ever lesson in karate.
The only thing worse than this would be to get involved in a fight with a little old lady and win.

Smile and be strong

There is a real reason to have fun. Having fun keeps us happy and balanced, so that we are in a stronger position to face challenges.

> *"The man who smiles is stronger than the man who grows angry."*
> Anon, The Little Book of Seishinkai

A friend of mine was the UK Junior Taekwondo champion. When he saw a video clip of me fighting when taking my Third Dan exam, he commented that I had adopted the strange tactic of blocking with my face!
This is a very advanced strategy, and I do not recommend it. Do NOT try this at home. In fact I hope that I never have to use it again.

Awareness

Work hard, have fun

There is a time to work hard, and a time to have fun. And it is perfectly OK to have fun whilst working hard. In the middle of a training session, my instructor, Malcolm Phipps, occasionally delivers one of his favourite lines, which you are welcome to use if this is relevant to you:

"The older I get the better I was."

When Black Belts get together we may 'talk shop' (about moves in a *kata*, different fighting strategies, or perhaps about breaking a technique down into small levels of detail) but we laugh. We have finished our training, we are aware of the importance of fun, we're out for a good time.

Black Belts know that having fun keeps us balanced and helps us maintain our zanshin.

One Thing You Can DO Now:

You have reached the end of this first section, so put the book down, and go and do something that you find FUN.

You know that everything starts with awareness.
You know how to have the awareness
of a Black Belt.

Strategy

I Karate DO

The full name for the martial art of karate is *karate-do*.

The '*do*' is pronounced 'dough'. It is not the 'doh' of Homer Simpson, it is the Japanese word meaning way. '*Budo*' means the way of the warrior. '*Judo*' means the way of peace. *Do*, the way, is HOW we get to where we want to be. It is the journey.

There is the WHY we do things, which we will look at in Strategy 8 *Bunkai*. And there is the WHAT we do, the actual activities, the specific actions.

The HOW is the link

It is the HOW that links the WHY and the WHAT.

WHY - - - -> HOW - - - -> WHAT

The HOW we get to where we want to be, the journey that takes us there, is so important.

Studies show that 70% of lottery winners lose everything within five years. Why? Because there is no journey. To suddenly arrive at the end destination of what was a long journey, which for many is financial security, is not what we are geared up for.

Our actual life itself is one big journey. And we don't want to reach the end of that particular journey too soon!

One journey, many journeys

Along the way we have things that we want to achieve, which are basically smaller journeys within our one big journey of life. We will cover Goals in a separate chapter. Goals are important; they give us focus and something to aim for. But HOW we get there is important, because:

If we don't enjoy the journey, we won't enjoy the destination.

Or, as in the case of lottery winners, when there is no journey, we won't be as content or happy as we think we will be. And we won't be able to adjust to our new situation, our new environment.

The goal, the journey

Sometimes the goal becomes more important than the journey. So that we achieve it at any cost, to us or others. This is not sustainable. Something somewhere is going to give. It could be our health; it could be a personal or business relationship. And when we arrive at the end of the journey it is not what we thought it was.

The shortest journey is not necessarily the best. It is along the journey that we learn new things, about ourselves and about others. This becomes our 'way'.

In karate, it is how Black Belts move during the performance of a technique that makes the technique work. It is the transition as we move from starting point A, to a transition point B, then perhaps to another transition point C, to the final destination D.

If the technique does not work at B or C, perhaps because the opponent has moved faster than we anticipated, it won't work at D. It is the journey that makes the technique, such as a block, punch or kick, work at D.

When we arrive at D we feel safe and secure, we know the technique is sound, and that it was effective all the way through, irrespective of what the opponent did.

This is just like the journeys of life. The gap between A and B, between B and C, and between C and D may be just a few tenths of a second (if we are doing a karate move), or it may be minutes, days, weeks, months or years. But the principle is the same.

As we go on our journey we want to feel safe and secure. We are aware of the end destination, but our focus is on the next part, which is B. As we get to B, we then focus on getting to C, and so on, knowing that at each stage we are effective, we are prepared for any eventuality, we are comfortable with where we are.

And when we arrive at our end destination, whatever that may be for that particular journey, we know that things have 'worked'. We know that we feel complete, that the journey has been worthwhile. We may have learned things along the way, or perhaps become aware of some new element that will help us improve our future performance. Or maybe we just had some fun.

Strategy and business

In business the HOW is the strategy, and these concepts apply here. It is how we achieve our goals and objectives, with the resources that we have.

RESOURCES - - - -> STRATEGY - - - -> OBJECTIVES/GOALS

Having *zanshin* and being aware of the importance of the journey will give a business even more flexibility, and the ability to spot threats and opportunities.

This will make a business more immune to competition. It is far more difficult for a competitor to imitate your strategy than the obvious sales and marketing activities and tactics that they will naturally be aware of.

"All men can see these tactics whereby I conquer, but what none can see is the strategy out of which victory is evolved."
Sun Tzu

Black Belts know that the journey, the way that we get to where we want to be, is important. Being aware of HOW we do things and enjoying the journey will mean we enjoy arriving at the destination even more.

One Thing You Can DO Now:

Think of a journey you are on. It might be in your personal life, something to do with your business, or something else such as a sport or a hobby. Where are you on the journey? Are you enjoying it? What would make it better?

2 System

For each journey we are on, each part of our way, we can break it down into smaller parts.

Black Belts break down an individual technique into smaller parts. For example, when we punch, we take into account:

The direction of the feet
Where the feet are placed
The rotation of the hips
The angle of the torso
BOTH arms
The direction we are looking at
The timing of the technique
Our breathing
Any change in balance during the execution of the technique
Where we focus
Awareness of the transition stages on the 'journey'
...and many more factors!

We focus on these individually, making sure that each part is doing what it should be doing and that the timing is right. We then put them back together, and we have a good technique.

These small parts are our system for delivering effective techniques. Techniques that work in any situation.

In life and in business, we can break down all our journeys, all the things we want to achieve, into smaller parts. These parts become our system.

We control our systems

The key things about the systems we have for delivering effective performance, performance that will help us achieve our goals, is that we control them.

The systems might be wrong, they might need changing, but we can control this.

And once we know we have a system that works, we just work our systems! Just the very nature of breaking things down, breaking them into smaller

Strategy

steps that are more manageable, is a successful strategy.

I recently worked with some financial advisors. They were keen to grow their businesses, so they wanted more clients. For each of them we came up with a system that gave them more contacts, made them more resilient to failure and setbacks, and more motivated to do the actual activity.

In other words, we came up with a system, of small steps, of daily activities, for:

LinkedIn – approaching contacts from previous jobs and roles, and THEIR contacts

Collecting rejections, because the more rejections they collected, the more 'yesses' they got

Rewarding themselves, based on their weekly activity, not their results

They felt in control. It was their system (it was different for each of them). And as they applied the system and started to get results, they knew how much of each part of the system they needed to do, to get the results they wanted.

Let's say you were about to start revising for a big exam. All the revision you would need to do might appear daunting. But once you start breaking it down into manageable chunks, and have a system for doing each small chunk, it will appear more manageable and more achievable. And you would feel more confident about passing, so you would be more motivated to do the revision!

Systems reduce uncertainty

In some hospitals, surgeons are encouraged to use a system of lists to check that everything is OK before they start operating. This system of lists has been shown to cut deaths during operations by up to 40%.

In business, systemising the activities of the business is a key factor for success.

Six Sigma is a methodology that improves business processes. It was first used at Motorola in 1986, and is now used worldwide to improve quality and cut defects in manufacturing and business processes.

A Six Sigma Black Belt is someone who has a thorough understanding of

ALL aspects of the methodology, and can address and correct a problem in any part of the business.

In the quality control of business processes AND the martial arts, Black Belts know that the way to improve performance in the overall process is to break things down into separate parts and look at them individually.

Why is breaking things down into small steps so effective? Because of the saying:

> "It's the difference that makes the difference."

Let's assume in your business you were to make two cold calls a day to potential prospects. Most of the time you wouldn't get through to the intended person. You wouldn't even have a conversation with a human being.But with over 500 calls a year, you WOULD have some conversations, and quite possibly get some new clients. So all you need is a system to make two cold calls a day, and you will grow your business.

In other words, just doing something makes things happen. Even small things. So taking one small step at a time will take us further along on the journey.

Black Belts use the proven strategy of breaking a technique down into its constituent parts to deliver effective techniques that work.

One Thing You Can DO Now:

Think of a big goal or challenge you are facing right now. How many parts can you break it down into? Take one of these parts, and decide on the next thing, however small, you can do easily. The smaller the better.

3 Goals

Many years ago, in ancient Japan, a 10 year old boy travelled to the home of a very famous swordsman because he wished to be taught the art of swordsmanship.

He was thrilled to be given an audience with the master. They sat down together, and the master said to the boy to ask any questions he liked. The boy asked, "Master, how long will it take me to become the finest swordsman in the land?"

The master replied, "Ten years."

The boy was a bit taken aback. He hadn't thought it would take this long. So the boy asked, "Master, if I train twice as hard as all the other students, how long will it take?"

The master thought for a while, and then replied, "Twenty years".

Twenty years! The boy could not imagine being 30 years old (because that's really old right?).

So the boy asked, "Master, if I train every single day, as soon as I wake up, until when I go to bed, and I train harder than any other student has ever trained, then how long will it take?"

The master thought, and then replied, "Thirty years".

The boy was now totally confused. He asked the master, "Master, how is it that every time I say I will train harder, you say it will take me longer?"

The master without hesitating replied, "The answer is clear. When there is one eye fixed upon the destination, there is only one eye left with which to find the way."

Goals are good. They give us focus, something to aim for, so that we learn as we go on our journey, and reward ourselves and perhaps others when we get there.

But we can be too focused on the goal, on the end of that particular journey.

Only I in 20 succeed

Most people who start karate aim to become a Black Belt. History shows that at best only one in 20 people will achieve this. Having a goal, in itself, guarantees nothing. And focusing on a goal can be counter-productive.

A different plan would be to have the goal of becoming a Black Belt, and to realise that in order to get to grading for the Black Belt, the 10th Belt, you would need to pass the 9th belt. And in order to grade for the 9th belt, you would need to have passed the 8th belt. And so on, working back.

It works all the way back to NOW. From NOW, from here, as a beginner, a White Belt needs to focus on what they need to do to get their first belt, the Red Belt.

So a good goal would be to know what they need to focus on this week, so that when they do the grading exam for Red Belt in a few weeks or months' time, they will be able to pass.

Carefully define your goals

The actor in Harry Potter I mentioned in Awareness 2 Self and Responsibility DID get his Black Belt. At the first attempt.

And he never trained again! His goal was to get his Black Belt, to help him in his acting career. He had achieved his goal, so he stopped. Because that was his goal, that was the right thing for him.

Black Belt is not a destination. It is only part of the journey.

One of the financial advisors I mentioned previously set himself an ambitious goal for 2014. He hit his goal for the year! On the 30th December 2014, with just two days of the year remaining. He told me he felt happy for 2 days, then realised he had to start all over again!

So he was an unhappy, under-achieving, goal-focused professional, who was happy for 2 days out of 365. Surely there has to be another way?

Small, slow and gentle

One of the most famous Black Belts ever in the history of judo (the way of peace) was a scientist and engineer called Moshe Feldenkrais. He wasn't famous for judo, but for the system he devised (called Feldenkrais), of movement, balance, posture and co-ordination. The Feldenkrais Method ® aims to help with pain, breathing, performance, and vitality.

A key part of the success of Feldenkrais is down to the small, slow, gentle movements and the lack of a goal. Feldenkrais practitioners, and their patients, focus on the process, not the goal.

The ultimate goal of karate is the perfection of the character of its participants. When Gichin Funakoshi, the founder of modern-day karate, was asked to explain this, the word he used was humility.

This is a very clever answer. We can never say we have attained humility. Perhaps others can say this about someone else, but by its very nature, we cannot say it about ourselves. It is something to be worked towards. (Humility is covered in much more detail in a future section.)

So it is a journey that lasts a lifetime. A journey rich in experience and understanding and development of self, where we never know if we have achieved our goal!

Goals are not within our Circle of Life. In other words, we do not control them. But we do control our systems.

Black Belts focus on the here and now. In a fight we focus on what is directly in front of us, the next challenge, the next obstacle, the next opportunity. This zanshin approach to our goals means that we focus on the things in our Circle of Life, the things that we control.

One Thing You Can DO Now:

Think of one big goal, break it down into its separate parts, and do something NOW that will help you achieve that particular part.

4 How Do You?

*"When you attain the way of strategy there will not be
one thing you cannot see."*
Miyamoto Musashi (undefeated swordsman from 17th Century Japan)

We have a strategy for EVERYTHING. For every single thing we do.
From the moment when we wake up in the morning, we are running our strategies, the HOW we do what we do. We are running them whether we are aware of them or not.
We have a strategy for waking up.
We have a strategy for getting out of bed (assuming we have been asleep in a bed).
We have a strategy for how we brush our teeth (assuming we brush our teeth!).
We have strategies for how we start our car, manage our emails, cross the road.
If we didn't have strategies, our brains would need to be the size of a planet. We would need to work out, from scratch, HOW we do everything thing that we do. Every second of every day.
For example, when we saw a pencil that we wanted to pick up, we would have to work out HOW we pick up pencils in general, and that pencil in particular. Or when we sat in our car, we would have to work out how and in what order to do the things we need to do to start the car moving.

We have strategies for everything
As well as having strategies for practical, daily activities, we also have and run other types of strategies. And this is where it gets interesting.
For example, we have strategies for how we feel loved. There will be certain things that, because of previous experiences and past behaviour, make us feel loved.
And if we are in a loving relationship with someone, they will also have strategies for how they feel loved!
And there could be hundreds of different things that make up their strategy for HOW they feel loved.

It might be receiving small gifts, or a big present, or planning future holidays with their partner, or having help with the chores around the house, or their partner providing enough money to make them feel secure, or holding hands together at every opportunity, or receiving texts saying 'I love you', or being complimented on their appearance, or being allowed to win an argument. Or any one of hundreds of ways.

Now we could guess the strategy by which our partner feels loved. After all, we know our partners pretty well, right?

Ask to find the strategy

What is the best way to find our partner's strategy for how they feel loved? Ask them! Ask them HOW they know they are loved. And don't necessarily expect an answer straight away. This is a powerful question to ask. To get a sensible, meaningful answer may take a bit of thought.

But imagine being with a partner, who you love and who you want to show that you love, that you knew the strategies which make them feel loved! What would a relationship like that look like?

Strategies and business

We can also use this concept in our business lives.

A lot of sales training focuses on selling strategies. After all, your selling strategies are within your circle, you control them.

Maybe this is a time to go outside your circle. Remember we mentioned getting to the point where you are comfortable being uncomfortable?

This is a good time to get uncomfortable, to get outside YOUR circle, and get in to theirs.

To a prospect, you could ask a question such as "When you are about to start dealing with a new supplier of (whatever it is you provide), how do you decide on the things/factors that make this a success for you? What do you take into consideration when choosing a new supplier who will be a good fit for your company?"

To an existing customer, who you want to carry on supplying, perhaps because you believe your business is under threat from a competitor, you could ask "How do you maintain an excellent relationship with your existing suppliers so that this continues to be a success for you and them?"

To an existing customer who you are selling a new product or service to, you could ask "How do you go about choosing new products from suppliers, so that this is a success for you?"

To an employer at a job interview you could ask "How do you choose the candidates that have the qualities that mean that you employ the right people who will make you even more successful?"

Whether in our personal lives or in business, being aware of our own strategies and the other people involved means we will be happier and more successful, and they will too.

Black Belts know that understanding other people's strategies is key.

One Thing You Can DO Now:

Think of a relationship that you care about, personal or in business, and think of a 'How Do You' question that you could ask.

5 Mapping Over

Knowing our own strategies is essential to come to a fuller understanding of who we are. It will give us a greater awareness of us.

Once we know HOW we do certain types of things, the strategy we have for how we do them, we can map this over to other areas, to make us more successful and make things easier.

I have used this with my karate students.

When the Harry Potter actor was getting nervous about his Black Belt Grading exam, we talked about whether he was nervous when being filmed. And he wasn't. Even though he was on a very expensive set, with actors who were becoming world famous, and had been practising for the 'big day', preparing for hours with his costume and make-up, and waiting for everyone else to be ready.

A bit like a Black Belt grading (although we don't wear make-up).

So we talked through his routine for getting ready to do some filming. He consciously went through his routine, increasing his awareness of his 'getting-ready-without-stress strategy'. And on the day of the Black Belt grading he ran his strategy, he was not nervous, and he passed first time.

Another of my karate students was a Black Belt at the age of 16. He would go on to become a Second Dan Black Belt and compete in major competitions.

But he was having problems at school, because he had difficulty focusing on his homework.

So we talked about how he focused when training in karate, and also when practising at home (which he did a lot of). We talked about how around his bedroom wall he told me he had put up sayings in Japanese, and posted up all the certificates from previous gradings.

So his strategy for focusing was to immerse himself in the environment, and remind himself of his previous successes and achievements.

He then did this with his school work, passed his exams and went to college to continue his studies.

Strategies from other areas

So if you are finding something a bit difficult, take a step back. Think of what strategies you could apply from other areas of your life where you have been successful.

For example, I have realised that when I learn something new, something that is not necessarily complicated, but long, I have a strategy.

And I became aware of this strategy when I thought how I learn new music to play on the piano, so that I know it off by heart, without the music in front of me. The strategy I run is:

- Listen to the piece so that I know how it goes
- Learn in small chunks
- Always start playing from the beginning, even when I am about 80% of the way through.

When I learn a *kata* in karate, (or just remind myself of the *kata* that I DO know) what I do is: Watch clips of the *kata* on YouTube so I know the overall form of the movements.

- Break it down into sets, each of a few moves
- Most of the time, start at the first move so I know where I am in the *kata*.

So I have a strategy for how I learn new things that are quite 'chunky', that are a bit involved.

Strategies for learning, losing weight...

If you are having a problem with learning something, how have you successfully learned to do other things? How did you learn to drive, or use your computer, or revise for an exam? What parts of this can you apply to the thing you are having a problem with?

If you are having a problem with losing weight, have you ever lost weight before, and if so how did you do it? What have you achieved that involved changing your daily habits? Do you have a strategy for denying yourself things you like (which can be a good thing), or delaying gratification? Or maybe rewarding yourself in a completely different way (so that you are not sabotaging your goal, for example by eating chocolate)? Do you have a strategy for making yourself accountable, either just to yourself, or do you tell others about your goals so that you are accountable to them? Have you made a big change which depended on you doing just one small thing at a time, and if so what was your strategy, how did you do it?

Black Belts know that one way to overcome problems, and increase our understanding of ourselves, is to map over strategies that we have used successfully in other areas of our lives.

One Thing You Can DO Now:

Think of a problem you are having right now or something you would like to achieve or do better. What successful strategies from other parts of your life might be relevant here? Think about successful strategies that you can map over and apply to this particular issue.

6 Modelling

When I was aged 7 at Primary School, I wanted to run fast. But I was a slow runner. One day in the school canteen I was behind two boys who were good runners. As we got to the serving hatch, I could see what foods they were choosing.

So I ate what they ate.

Although my running never got as fast as theirs, I now realised that I was applying the strategy of modelling. Even before I consciously knew what it was!

Modelling is where we mimic the actions of someone whose performance we want to achieve. We want to achieve the results they are getting, so we copy their actions and behaviour.

Copy the best

A very famous karate instructor told how, as he was developing his skills, he looked around his *Dojo* and looked at the Black Belts. He went to competitions, where he worked out the strengths of the main competitors. He wanted the speed of X, the spirit of Y and the reflexes of Z. He took all these separate parts, modelled them, and became a top competitor, and later on a coach for the England Karate Squad. He copied the top performers and became one himself.

Top sports people and top business people do this.

We can do this.

If there is someone whose performance we want to copy, we model their behaviour. We do what they do.

Formula One drivers are superbly fit, very careful about that they eat and drink, and have a massage to loosen up just before getting in the car to start the race. If you were aiming to become a top world-class Formula One driver, ate loads of pizza and burgers, drank alcohol, never exercised and made a point of getting in to a car really stiff and inflexible, you're almost certainly not going to get there. Regardless of your skill level.

But by modelling the behaviour of top performing drivers, you would have a chance.

Research the top performers

If there is something you want to achieve, find out about people who have already done it. What are they like? What do they eat? How much do they invest in personal development? What qualifications do they have? What is their work ethic? Find out everything you can about them and copy it.

Modelling is a strategy that we can use that is empowering. We can copy anyone.

And if we don't want to live like them 100%, we just model the parts that will be of use to us, that will help us get to where we want to go.

Black Belts continue to improve their performance by copying the actions and behaviour of top performers.

One Thing You Can DO Now:

Think of one thing you want to achieve, look at who is already doing it, and start copying some or all of their actions and behaviour.

7 Rapport

Samurai warriors only ever carried their swords on their left hand side, at the hip, attached to the belt around their waist.

This is because *Samurai* warriors were right handed. It is more natural for the right hand to draw a weapon from the left hip than from the right.

When we shake hands with our right hand, we are showing that we are not carrying a weapon, that we are not about to attack them with a bladed weapon.

Trust

This builds rapport, because we are showing that we trust the other person.

If you are ever doing a presentation, have your palms up. This shows you are not carrying a weapon, so builds rapport.

In sales and business meetings, make sure your hands are on the table, that the other people in the meeting can see them. This builds rapport (assuming you are not showing you are carrying a knife!).

When we build rapport, we can have deeper, more meaningful, trusting relationships. In our personal lives and in our business lives.

Go with

I did some work with Charlene, who sold insurance over the phone. Her conversion rate was 20%, compared to the average in her office of 30%.

We spent about 20 minutes discussing the strategy of building rapport, and her conversion rates increased to 30%, and stayed at 30%. That's a 50% increase! She built rapport by setting the scene with the people she was calling.

So if, for example, she had been provided their name and contact details by a web site, she explained how she had been given their details, what the call was about, and why this could be good for them. She then went into her normal script. The only change she had made was that she built rapport from the start.

In martial arts this strategy can be referred to as 'Go with.'

In some situations, 'go with' takes the fight out of the other person. It builds rapport, as we become to some extent a mirror of the other person.

Strategy

I was once in a karate competition, fighting a higher grade who was smaller but much faster and more agile than me. As we started to fight, I couldn't get near him. He was keeping out of range of my longer arms, sometimes moving a bit nearer, then a bit further away, then off to one side, then towards me a bit, then out, and so on. I was getting tired just watching him! No contact was made. The 'fight' went on. Then I felt his fist in my throat. It was perfectly controlled and I wasn't hurt (except my pride). It was the first contact we had made. He had won.

There was no rapport. There was a young, small, agile Black belt who moved around a lot. And there was me – older, bigger, and much less agile. The only chance I had would have been to move around as much as him. I should have gone with him.

When we 'go with' someone we build rapport (and tend not to get hit in the throat).

Having a problem with someone who is ridiculing you? One option is to go with them. Just agree. Say "Yes, I'm rubbish at..." Or "Oh yes, I am always doing that." Don't mentally agree, just verbally go with them.

If you go with them, verbally, they have nothing to fight.

In this type of situation another option we can choose is to go beyond going with them! This will either stop the negative situation, or provoke another reaction. (Check you are OK for this reaction to happen, and use your *zanshin* to be ready just in case.)What we can do is to exaggerate what they are saying. You are mocking their mockery, mimicking their mimicry. They have nowhere else to go with that particular technique.

Black Belts know that one strategy they can choose to adopt is to go with the other person, to build trust and rapport.

One Thing You Can DO Now:

Think of someone you would like a closer, more trusting relationship with, and build rapport with them by showing trust and mirroring one aspect of their behaviour.

8 Bunkai (Listen for the Why)

A strategy to give us awareness of the real meaning that lies behind something, is *Bunkai*.

In *kata*, some of the moves that we do have no obvious application. It is difficult at first to see how they could be useful in a real-life situation.

The *Bunkai* gives us the WHY we perform a particular move in a particular way.

The move might actually be an arm lock, a take-down or throw, or evasion of a particular attack where we set ourselves up for a strong counter-attacking move.

The real reason

It is the real reason we do the move.

When we do the *kata* move, and know and understand the *Bunkai*, everything makes sense.

When we are communicating with someone, in our personal lives or in business, the real meaning of what they are saying is not always obvious. It would help us, and them, if we could understand what they are actually saying. And show to them that we have understood.

Active listening

One strategy to do this is active listening.

Firstly, it is important to listen!

And to listen with no intent of responding. You may have heard the phrase, which can be posed as a question:

> "Are you listening to respond or to receive?"

'Listening to respond' is where someone appears to be listening, but actually is only waiting for the other person to breathe in. As soon as they do, the 'listening to respond' person immediately takes advantage of the pause to say what they are focusing on. Which is probably not what the other person was talking about. And they have not been really listening to

Strategy

the other person.

We have one mouth and two ears.

But when we listen to receive, we are totally focused on the other person and what they are saying. We are living in the moment, with high *zanshin*, aware of every word. This way we can understand what they are saying, and why they are saying it. We can understand the real meaning, the *Bunkai*, of their words.

Secondly, it is important that we actually show that we are listening.

A good strategy here is to occasionally summarise what the other person has been saying.

We can do this in a variety of ways:

- We can summarise everything they have said in to one or two sentences
- We can repeat a phrase
- We can just repeat a key word

The most effective strategy is to summarise everything they have said, as this shows we have been listening all the time!

This strategy of summarising can be in used in business, in sales, in job interviews, and in our personal lives. It builds rapport and trust, and it shows that we care about what they are saying, that we care about them.

Thirdly, doing more active listening gives us more of an opportunity to learn something new. Something that we can take from the other person's journey that may be helpful to us on our own journey.

> *"When you talk, you are only repeating what you know;*
> *But when you listen, you may learn something new."*
> The Dalai Lama

Black Belts know that by listening actively we can understand the other persons Bunkai, the why of what they are saying, resulting in intelligent, productive conversations for both parties.

One Thing You Can DO Now:

Plan that in your next communication, you will show that you are actively listening, either by summarising, repeating a phrase, or a key word.

Strategy

9 Objections

We can face objections in all areas of our lives. Sometimes they are justified, raising valid concerns that could mean we are in danger (or we are about to do something daft!).

And sometimes they are not justified, or are only representing one person's view, when ours is equally valid.

We can face objections in business, especially in a sales environment, as well as in our personal lives.

Fighting strategies, proven over hundreds of years, give us some options to deal with objections. Both reactively, in terms of dealing with an objection that has been raised, and proactively, in dealing with them before they come up.

Miyamoto Musashi was an undefeated swordsman from 17th Century Japan. To be undefeated when every fight was to the death, and to die of old age in his sixties (which was old for that era) tells us just how good he was.

Three ways to handle objections

His *Book of Five Rings* (also called *Go Rin No Sho*) is a classic book of martial arts strategy. In the book there are three strategies to 'forestall an enemy':

Tai No Sen   This is where the 'enemy' attacks, and we block. So we are attacked with an objection, and we deal with it successfully. This is OK, but it is reactive.

Tai Tai No Sen This is where we meet the enemy's attack, the other person's objection, with a counter attack. If we were negotiating, we could say "Yes I am happy to give you X, on the basis that we can agree Y is (whatever you want Y to be)". Or in sales for example, we could say something like "I am happy to discuss pricing, but can we agree that if we resolve this issue that you will go ahead and place an order?" This tells you if there are any other attacks (objections) that may be coming in, so you know what you are fighting against. This is a stronger strategy than *Tai No Sen*, and is known in sales as the Conditional Close, but again it is reactive.

Ken No Sen   We 'attack'. Although this is the first of Musashi's fighting strategies, when dealing with objections it gives us a powerful option, where we take the fight to the other person. Here, we bring up the possible objection, even before it has been mentioned. And perhaps even before it has come up in the mind of the other person! This shows confidence and rapport, in that we are thinking of them. So we could say something like "If I was you, right now I'd be thinking that the pricing is too high" (as an example). And then go on to give your reasons why the pricing is right. Or in a job interview, you could say "If I was you I would be thinking their last job is not that relevant to the role advertised, so let me tell you some of my duties and achievements that are very relevant to why I am here today." Used correctly this is a very effective strategy, because it is pro-active.

Another option is just to agree with their objection. As we discussed in Strategy 7 Rapport, we can 'go with' the other person, agreeing to their objection, giving them nothing to fight. We don't even block or counter, we just agree.

This might not be a strategy we want to use on big issues, but on smaller points we have an option to just give way. Remember the old saying of 'pick your battles?' This is an option to be considered occasionally. From a negotiating point of view, remember that this strategy is conceding something without asking for anything in return, which is not classic negotiating. But it can be a useful strategy for keeping things peaceful! Pick your battles. Pick your fights. As Robin Williams said:

"Never pick a fight with an ugly person, they've got nothing to lose."

Strategy

Black Belts know that although they can deal with most attacks, the most effective strategy is to 'take the fight to the enemy', by raising their concerns first, thus avoiding having to fight.

One Thing You Can DO Now:

Think of someone who may have an objection to something you have said or done, and plan when you will raise it with them, in a friendly conciliatory way, thus taking the heat out of the situation and avoiding future conflict.

10 Culture And Patterns

Our culture, for ourselves, in the groups we belong to, whether at home, socially, in business or professionally, includes all the knowledge, experience, values and strategies of the group.
An indication of the culture of karate is given from the inside of my Karate Licence, which reads:

> *"I promise to uphold the true spirit of Karate-Do and never to use the skills that I am taught against persons, except for the defence of myself, family or friends in the instance of extreme danger, or in support of law and order."*

This is in alignment with the gravestone of *Sensei* Gichin Funakoshi, which reads:

> *Karate ni sente nashi*
> (There is no first attack in karate)

So the culture of karate is that it is not to be used aggressively, unilaterally. And that it will only be used in the right circumstances.

Insight into a culture
How do we get an insight into a culture?
One insight into a culture, to increase our awareness of our own culture or of a particular group we belong to, is to look for patterns.
A pattern is a type of behaviour we produce in different areas. Seeing patterns can also give us insights and more understanding of ourselves and others.
Patterns of behaviour can be at the personal level. Here, when they are negative, we get caught in a circle, always recreating the same problems and failures. Examples include:

- Always selecting partners who have the same types of negative behaviour. At the extreme, this includes people who have chosen several partners who have abused them.
- Never completing things, whether something in the garden, a

work project, or reading a book.

- Frequently failing on personal goals, whether to do with health, fitness, weight, money, job or love and relationships.

One way to break out of this is to consider any common factors and then address them. For example, if we have a pattern of not completing things, had we visualised what it would look like when we had completed them? What was our motivation for starting them in the first place? Had we given enough time to that particular activity? Had we planned in advance so that we would be able to focus on that one thing? Had we planned our 'journey goals', to keep us motivated? Had we told others what we were doing, to increase our accountability? If we see any patterns, we can then address this part of our behaviour, as this could be the root cause of the pattern that we want to get rid of.

Black Belts look for patterns, in their own behaviour and others, to give an insight into their culture. Improving the culture improves the performance.

One Thing You Can DO Now:

Think of a particular type of behaviour you exhibited recently, either 'good' or 'bad', and look at other types of situations or other environments where you exhibited similar behaviour. Is there a common pattern? If so, plan how you will break out of it.

You know the importance of the journey and you know how to get to where you want to be. You have the strategy of a Black Belt.

Spirit

I Spirit Or Technique

The ONE thing that has been ingrained in me, over 28 years of karate is:

In a fight, spirit is more important than technique.

When things really matter, most of the techniques we have available will not be that relevant.
In a fight, most kicks won't work. I can't do head-high kicks wearing jeans or normal trousers. The distancing and angles won't be right for many types of punch or hand technique.

Adversity and 'failing'

In life, and in business, when we need support, when things go wrong, the single most important factor is our spirit. The vast majority of successful business people have overcome adversity. Usually they have had one or more 'failed' businesses or major hiccups in their career.
There are always times when it is easy to give up. To decide to fight no longer.
The thing that will carry us through tough times is our spirit.

"Your spirit is the true shield."
Morihei Ueshiba, founder of *Aikido*, in *The Art of Peace*

Muhammad Ali said it best:

"Champions aren't made in gyms. Champions are made from something they have deep inside of them, a desire, a dream, a vision. They have to have the skill, and the will. But the will must be stronger than the skill."

Ivan Misner, founder of BNI (Business Networking International), the world's largest referral marketing organisation and a Black Belt in karate:

"Ignorance on fire is better than knowledge on ice."

Mistakes? Who cares?

In karate gradings, you could make a few mistakes, and possibly still pass, as long as they weren't major errors.

You could possibly have one or two techniques that are not quite that sharp, and possibly, just possibly, still pass.

> A famous karate story tells how a beginner was taking their first grading exam, going for their Red belt, and grading the exam was the highest ever Karate instructor, 10th Dan Hirokazu Kanazawa.
>
> The beginner started their *kata*, a pre-arranged set of moves, which involves moving in different directions. After their third move, they needed to take one more step forwards, before reversing direction. But they had misjudged how near they were to the wall, and they were right at the edge of the hall. There was not enough space to do their fourth move.
>
> But directly ahead, right in front of them, was the door to a store cupboard.
>
> With one hand they opened the door, and completed the fourth move by stepping in to the cupboard! Where the examiner could not see their technique!
>
> They completed the *kata*. At the end, the people who had passed were announced. 'Cupboard man' passed! He had made a big mistake, but was still good enough to pass.

Spirit Spirit Spirit

If your spirit is poor, you will fail. Even if your techniques are brilliant and you make no mistakes.

If your spirit is good, and you make one or two mistakes, you might still pass.

Over the last 28 years I have learned quite a few powerful and effective techniques. There are 20 ways of using the hand as a weapon, there are six elbow techniques. But if I was ever to get involved in a fight, the most useful resource I would call upon is that for 28 years I have been training my spirit.

"Spirit first, technique second."
Sensei Gichin Funakoshi

This section is about how we can develop the spirit of a Black Belt. There are many techniques to help us, personally and in business. But it is our spirit that will help us on our journey, that will get us through the tough times, and be there when we need it most.

Black Belts know that spirit is more important than technique. When they train, they are aware that they are training their spirit, whatever techniques they are doing.

One Thing You Can DO Now:

Think of a challenging event or period of hardship in your life. What type of spirit did you demonstrate to get through it?

2 Down But Not Out

Everyone has times in their life when they are down. The most successful business women, the most successful sportsmen, people you know who just seem generally happy and content with their lives. Everyone has had to come through times when they were on the floor. Sometimes literally, sometimes metaphorically.

They are down. Down emotionally, physically, mentally, or financially.

Carry on fighting

But just because we are down, does not mean we are out. In karate workshops, I demonstrate being down and on the floor.

From being down on the floor, we have many options if we choose to fight on. There are all sorts of 'takedowns' we can perform using the legs. It is also fairly easy to protect our vital areas, by keeping our legs towards the attacker, so that they form a powerful line of defence.

We can easily absorb more attacks; even the strongest kick can be absorbed by using the arms in a relaxed way, where we absorb the impact of an attack rather than try to repel it.

So we CAN defend ourselves.

My favourite quote of all time is from Bruce Lee:

"To hell with circumstances, I create opportunities."

We can fight on! When we are down we are much nearer to one big vital area where the opponent, no matter how big and strong they are, is weak; their groin.

When I am demonstrating being down, lying on the floor, I ask for a volunteer to come and stand near me, to get ready to attack me. Just before they attack me I tell them there is one thing they need to know. That is, that with every remaining resource I have, even if it is the last thing I do on this earth, I plan to punch them very, very hard in the groin.

I then ask them if they would like to attack me!

Nobody ever has. It is the spirit of carrying on, of still being able to fight, that means they won't attack.

(Please note: this strategy applies one on one in a self-defence situation. If there is more than one attacker you need to get up quick, because one attacker will stay at your 'feet end', and another will go to your 'head end'. Here you can't see them, they only have your arms to contend with and they are nearer to your vital areas, and you would be in trouble.)

As well as being able to carry on fighting when we are down, the thing to do is to get up. There is a famous Japanese saying - Fall seven times, get up eight.

> *"Inside of a ring or out, there's nothing wrong with going down.*
> *It's staying down that's wrong."*
> Muhammad Ali

Black Belts know that in karate and in life there will be times when they are down. Things just haven't worked out as expected. In spite of high zanshin, something has come along and they are 'down'. They will get up and they will carry on.

One Thing You Can DO Now:

Think of the type of spirit from the previous chapter that you used to overcome a challenge in your life. How would you use this Black Belt spirit to overcome a challenge in the future?

3 The Power Of Beliefs

Beliefs are incredibly important. Beliefs, by their very nature, are things that we believe to be true. A belief is a feeling of certainty about something. Our beliefs are a key part of who we are.

Our beliefs can be positive, give us more spirit and empower us. Or they can be negative beliefs that drain our spirit and dis-empower us.

Placebo and nocebo

The power of beliefs is well documented in the medical world with the concept of a placebo. A placebo is a test treatment or 'medication' that is inert, but the patient has been told that it will help them, and therefore it has powerful positive effects.

There is also a nocebo. A nocebo is where symptoms worsen because a patient has been told, for the type of treatment or medication they are on, that they WILL get worse. Because they believe it to be true, it happens. Even though there is no medical reason why they would get worse.

Ageing as a belief

One of the best studies ever about the power of beliefs was done by Ellen Langer in 1979. Ellen Langer was a professor of Psychology at Harvard University. In a well-documented study that was to kick-start the anti-ageing industry, in 1979 she took a group of men in their 70's and 80's from a home in Boston (with their consent!) to a nearby retreat. The men lived as though it was 1959, 20 years earlier. So they were allowed to watch 'new' films such as Some Like It Hot, on a black and white television, but no film produced after that. The magazines they read, and everything to do with their environment, was as if it was 1959, which they referred to in the present tense.

After one week, there were startling improvements in the men's physical and medical conditions.

Because they were starting to believe they were 20 years younger, their bodies were adapting!

Another group of men of similar age who went to a similar retreat and lived in the present time of 1979, showed some improvement, but not as significant as the 59ers.

So our beliefs are very powerful. Maybe the belief that we have to get old, get ill, and die, does not have to be 100% true all the time. What other beliefs are we carrying, that we unaware of, that are affecting our lives?

Beliefs and negative emotions

As we saw in Awareness 3 Being Present, by being present we can avoid or minimise some powerful negative emotions:

Past	Future
Guilt	Fear
Regret	Anxiety
B E L I E F S	

Beliefs underlie all these. Beliefs come from our past, and have a key effect on our future.

Beliefs and reality

But here's the key thing about beliefs. Beliefs are not reality! Beliefs are generalisations about past experiences that are often based on a misinterpretation of the reality at the time. Beliefs meander around our bodies disguised as the truth.

When we stay comfortable, when we stay in our comfort zone, our Circle of Life, we do not challenge our beliefs. By making a conscious effort to get out of our comfort zone, we can challenge beliefs that may be holding us back.

Black Belts are aware of a belief that could be limiting them. They will challenge it, even if it means getting uncomfortable, getting outside their comfort zone.

One Thing You Can DO Now:

Think of something you would like to do, something that maybe you have wanted to do for a while. What is it that is stopping you? Could this be a limiting belief?

4 Limiting Beliefs

I was teaching a karate lesson which had a mixture of students. There were two Black Belts, some experienced junior grades, and Keith.

Keith was 55, a diabetic with a heart condition and other ailments. When he had turned up for his first lesson a couple of months ago, I asked him why he wanted to learn karate. He replied that he wanted to be at his grandson's wedding, even if he was to be in a wheelchair. So he needed to lose weight and get fitter.

He was making progress in his training, but had a major problem. He could not first raise his knee in order to do a front snap kick. If the knee does not raise, the kick at the moment of impact is going straight upwards. But when we focus on first raising the knee, and then do the kick, the foot travels horizontally from its raised position, and will therefore be effective. It will have impact.

I had tried everything I could think of.

The room where we were training had a set of solid wooden steps leading up to a stage. On a whim, I asked Keith to stand at the bottom of the steps. Then I asked him to put his foot on the bottom step, with his leg out straight. After about 15 seconds he put his foot on the next step. And after a while, on the next, and then on the fourth step.

His knee and foot were now at the right height for the kick! He COULD do it. He lined up with the class to resume training. His next kick was the best kick he had ever done.

Why?

Because he now believed he could do it!

He had the belief that he COULD raise his knee and execute a powerful, effective front snap kick. Nothing else had changed. His legs and hips had not miraculously loosened up. It was the belief that he could do it that made him be able to do it.

I have a question for you:

Are you kicking too low?

Punch above your weight, kick above your height

Is there some aspect of your life where you see or know of other people who are achieving something that you want in your life? It doesn't have to be anything material, it could be hanging out with a group of good friends, always being happy, never showing anger.

The three problems with beliefs are known as the Three Ps. Beliefs are:

Permanent – if we don't do anything to challenge or change them, they will stay with us

Pervasive – they affect all areas of our body and mind, and therefore our life

Personal – they are ours, which makes it difficult to be aware of them (but not for Black Belts with their *zanshin*!)

But we CAN change limiting beliefs.

Questioning our beliefs

Once we are aware of them, the first thing is to question the belief.

Just by questioning the belief, we create doubt about it. Doubt that it applies 100% of the time, in every situation.

And the moment we start to question a belief, it starts to lose its hold over us. As an example, let's look at cold calling. Most people do not like making cold calls. The vast majority of cold calls don't work. We don't get through to the right person, sometimes we cannot even find out who the right person is. Then, when we finally do get to speak with the right person, they don't want to talk, or fob us off by asking us to send an email.

If 100% if cold calls were to fail, all the time, there would be no point.

I did some calls for a training company. About 97% of the calls 'failed'. Which meant 3% worked! I was happy to carry on making calls. I made a few hundred calls, and the company got some good new clients.

As soon as our certainty drops below 100%, we are in the game! So just by the very nature of questioning a belief, we are saying to ourselves that it might not apply 100% of the time.

When Keith started putting his foot on higher and higher steps, he was questioning his belief.

Pain

Another way to change a limiting belief is to associate it with pain. Ask ourselves what is this belief stopping me from doing? What other negative effects is it having? What pain is it causing me?

This then motivates us to do something about it.

Black Belts know that by challenging limiting beliefs they will keep their spirit high.

One Thing You Can DO Now:

Think of something you have been trying to achieve, something that you know can be done, then consider what is stopping you. This could indicate a limiting belief, which you can start to question. What pain is this belief causing?

5 Self-Talk

Self-talk is the talk that we have within our heads. It is ours and ours alone. No one else can hear it. Which is sometimes a good thing! But which also means our self-talk is very powerful, because no one else can challenge it. What we say to ourselves affects how we feel, it affects our actions and our behaviour.

> An old karate master was teaching a children's class, when suddenly he asked them to come and sit down around him, because he had a story to tell them.
> He shocked them by telling them that inside each of them there were two tigers! And the tigers were fighting with each other.
> One tiger represented all the things that were good in life, such as honesty, courage, hope, love, and peace.
> The other tiger represented all the things that were bad in life, such as hatred, jealousy, anger, and betrayal.
> The children were quiet for some time (which in my experience is very rare in a children's class!) as they thought about the two tigers in each of them, fighting.
> Then one child asked "Master, which tiger will win?"
> The Master replied "The one you feed."

The problem with self-talk is that we can be feeding the 'bad' tiger, consciously or unconsciously.

Feeding our negative self-talk

Our limiting beliefs pop into our heads as negative self-talk. Which means no-one else becomes aware of them. So our limiting beliefs stay in our heads, feeding our negative tiger.

But limiting beliefs are like *ninjas*. *Ninjas* hide in dark places, and rarely show themselves.

Limiting beliefs hide at the back of our head, in the cerebellum, which means 'little brain'. Here it is dark, away from the light at the front of our brain, which is why it is difficult to see them. Once we have *zanshin* of these *ninjas* of limiting beliefs, we can attack them. And a Black Belt can defeat a *ninja*!

How can we overcome these *ninjas* of negative self-talk, these limiting beliefs that are dampening our spirit?

Attack the ninja

Here are six ways. The next time you have some negative self-talk, ask yourself: Am I over-generalising? If I am saying something like "This always happens", ask yourself "Does it really ALWAYS happen?"

1) Am I taking responsibility for something that is not my fault?
2) Am I stuck in 'all or nothing' thinking? Just because I haven't got everything, am I thinking I have got nothing?
3) Am I jumping to a (negative) conclusion when there is not really sufficient evidence?
4) Am I seeing it as a catastrophe, when actually it isn't?
5) Have I ignored the positive aspects?

And here is my favourite technique, for defeating the *ninjas* of negative self-talk and overcoming a negative belief:

Take the 't' out.

Kara ' e

Many negative words, the words we use in negative self-talk, have a 't' in them. Such as 'I can't' or 'I shouldn't'.

Take the 't' out! Turn it into 'I can', 'I should'.

And if you take the 't' out of 'I won't' you get 'I won'!

> Becki Wilson is the Managing Director at The Loft, an award-winning Brand and Digital Agency near Liverpool, England. She had a limiting belief that she was bad at presenting.
>
> "Nick, your 'Warrior Within' presentation at BNI Cheshire & North Wales Members Day had a very positive impact on me personally, inspired me to take action and to challenge a limiting belief that I held... As a result, the action I took saw me introducing a fashion

show at Wetherby Races, where some of the event was streamed live on Sky TV!"

Becki took out the 't' from "I can't present"which made it into "I can present". She defeated the *ninja* of negative self-talk and overcame her limiting belief.
Sometimes it can be just that simple.

Black Belts are aware of their self-talk, and if it is negative they defeat these negative ninjas and overcome their limiting beliefs. This keeps their spirit high.

One Thing You Can DO Now:

Be aware of negative self-talk by 'listening' out for words with a 't' in them. The next time you hear a 't', take it out!

6 Strengths

We all have weaknesses. And we all have strengths.
Black Belts play to their strengths. They largely ignore their weaknesses.

> One of the most formidable UK karate fighters ever was a senior instructor called Steve Cattle. He was respected by his peers, and competed internationally. He was part of the UK team captained by Terry O'Neill that won the 1975 World Championships in Los Angeles. But he had a weakness.
>
> Steve Cattle was short (for a karate fighter).
>
> If you are short, it is much more difficult to deliver effective kicks. When faced with taller opponents, you have to kick above YOUR height all the time!
>
> But Steve Cattle had a strength. He had very fast arms. His favourite technique was a snap of the elbow, attacking the opponents face. (The usual health warnings apply: do NOT try this at home.)
>
> People who he trained with said that they knew what was coming, they just didn't know when, because he was so fast.
>
> My instructor, Malcolm Phipps, said he never saw Steve Cattle throw a kick.
>
> Steve Cattle took on the best in the world, and won, by playing to his strength of having fast arms. He practiced and practiced using his very fast arms.

The uniqueness of strengths

The words strengths is unique. With nine letters, it is the longest word of one syllable in the English language.
And just as strengths is a unique word, your strengths are unique to you.
So how can we identify our strengths?
Here are three ways:

1. You may have won an award or received a certificate for something or passed an exam. If you have achieved one of these then you have one or more strengths.
2. If time seems to fly when you are doing a particular type of activity,

Spirit

and things just seem to come naturally to you. This indicates you have a strength.

3. Other people say that you are good at something. Sometimes, even with a high level of awareness, we don't see ourselves as well as other people do.

And it is important to continue to build on our strengths, to develop them and make them the best they can possibly be.

Why?

Developing our strengths

People who believe their strengths are innate, that their strengths are just natural to them, can face problems. Because when things go wrong, there is nothing extra they can do. If with their natural strengths they have got in to a negative situation, they will feel dis-empowered. They will believe there is nothing else they can do to improve the situation.

But if someone has worked on their strengths, when things go wrong they can continue to develop and build on their strengths, to overcome the problem. This is empowering.

In the corporate world, if a person is good at presenting but not so good, for instance, with spreadsheets, they are usually sent on a training course to improve their use of spreadsheets.

A better approach would be to send them on a presentation course. Then they may learn just one or two things that will make them an even better presenter. Someone else can do the spreadsheets!

Black Belts are aware of their strengths, and play to them.

One Thing You Can DO Now:

Identify one strength that you have, and think of a time when you will next apply it, a time when you might not have thought of using it.

7 Fail?

"Only a man who knows what it is like to be defeated can reach down to the bottom of his soul and come up with the extra ounce of power it takes to win when the match is even."
Muhammad Ali

When I went for my first Dan Black Belt, my instructor did not think I had reached the standard required. I 'failed'. I politely asked him what I needed to work on, and he told me three things. I worked on these three things for six months, retook the exam, and this time reached the required standard. I was now a Black Belt.

I knew that I had earned it, I knew that I had improved. I knew that it wasn't something that had just been given to me because I was an instructor of a club in a highly respected karate organisation. I knew that there was a standard, and that I had met it, at my second attempt. It meant a lot.

Two years later I went for my second Dan Black Belt. Again my instructor did not think I had reached the standard required, and I 'failed'. I again politely asked him what I needed to work on, and he told me three things. I worked on these three things for six months, retook the exam, and this time reached the required standard. I was now a Second Dan Black Belt.

So I have 'failed' twice. But, as I write this, I am 54 years old, a 4th Dan in karate, still plugging away, still teaching, training when I can, attending courses, and refereeing. Am I a failure in karate? You can decide.

Setbacks on our journey of life

This is just like life. We have 'failures'. We have setbacks. We have things that just don't go as planned.

These events are not exceptions to our life, our way, our journey. They are PART of the journey.

It is how we deal with them that counts.

Black Belts treat 'failure' as an opportunity to learn, to learn something about ourselves. This then becomes an important part of our way.

"Failure is the key to success;
Each mistake teaches us something."
Morihei Ueshiba

One strategy to not 'fail' is to pick your battles. Before you decide to do something, something that is going to take up your energy, you make a conscious decision whether to go in, or not. This way we develop great spirit, because when we have chosen to 'fight', we will give it everything. There is no 50%, or 90%, it is just all in or nothing.

Pierre Omidyar was one of the founders of eBay. He was a billionaire at the age of 31, and today runs the Omidyar Network, which invests for social impact.

When people come to him seeking funds, his first question is whether they have had a failure, a business that has failed. If the answer is No, he asks them to go away and fail before he gives them any money!

Life IS tough sometimes. But if we keep going, we'll never fail.

"If you're going through hell, keep going."
Winston Churchill

Black Belts never fail because they know you only fail if you give up.

One Thing You Can DO Now:

Think of something where you 'failed' and ask yourself what you learned and how you can apply this to your life in the future.

8 Ask Questions

Black Belts know that we have to ask questions.

We do this physically, when we are fighting. We attack, or feign an attack, to see what the response from the opponent will be.

This gives us clues about their strategy for defending, for how they move, for their favourite technique. We then use this information to give us an advantage.

We have already seen the importance of asking questions.

We ask questions to find someone's strategy – perhaps a strategy for how they feel loved, or how a business buys a product or service from a new supplier.

And we ask questions, of ourselves, to start dismantling a limiting belief.

Questions and answers

We will only get answers when we start asking questions.

And if we get the wrong answers, it might be because we are asking the wrong questions!

Think of asking questions as an attack, or as a feint. You are eliciting a response from the other person, you are learning something about them that might be useful.

So to all your employees, customers, friends, loved ones, suppliers etc – attack them!

Well, maybe just ask them questions.

Good sales people ask lots of questions.

What do you want?

Ask for what you want. Children are good at this; it is a skill that we can lose as we get older.

When I failed my first two Dan gradings, I asked what I needed to do to reach the required standard. I was told what I needed to do, so I went and did it. Simple.

Is there something you want? Have you asked for it? Or at least have you asked someone what you need to do to get it? Or asked someone who is the right person to go and ask for it?

Many things in life, the good things, don't just naturally come to us. We have to go and get them. Asking questions is one way of getting them.

Initiative

When you ask questions, you maintain the initiative. You're the one dictating the conversation, getting the other person thinking. You have some degree of control, and in a conversation you appear to be interested in them, which builds rapport.

Asking questions shows spirit. You are in the arena, you are the one going forwards, making a contribution, setting the pace.

Black Belts ask questions of others, and are happy to ask for what they want.

One Thing You Can DO Now:

Is there something you want, and do you know who you can ask for it? If so, go and ask for it.

9 Practising

"The fight is won or lost far away from witnesses,
behind the lines, in the gym, and out there
on the road, long before I dance under those lights."
Muhammad Ali

In karate, practising is essential. As well as training twice or more a week, keeping a diary, watching videos and everything else. One of my instructors told me that I could get to Black Belt with three minutes a day! Three minutes a day!
That's practising for three minutes every day, plus training.

It's the extra that counts
It is the 'little and often' approach that gets people to Black Belt. Doing something a bit extra, something that other people are not doing.
David Beckham used to go and do his daily training with his team mates. After the training had finished he would go and find a set of goal posts, and suspend a tyre so it was hanging from one corner of the goal. Then he would practice his free kicks, aiming to get every ball in the tyre.
It is the practising that gives us that little bit extra. That little bit of extra skill, that little bit more of developing a natural strength.

Keep the water boiling
Practising regularly keeps our skills sharp, and our strengths strong.

"Karate is like boiling water; without heat, it returns to its tepid state."
Gichin Funakoshi

The training and the practising need to be continuous. Training and practising hard for two weeks, then having two weeks of rest, does not work.
This is just like having a system to achieve our goals. It is the small steps, the three minutes a day, EVERY day, that will get us to Black Belt.
Our brains like constant practice! Donald Hebb, a Canadian neuropsychologist, came up with the phrase 'neurons that fire together

Spirit

wire together'. Every feeling, thought and action that we do is stored in some of the 100 billion nerve cells in our brain (neurons).Every time we repeat that feeling, thought or action, the same neurons fire, so we keep strengthening the connection between these neurons in our brain. Ultimately we arrive at the martial art state of *mushin*, meaning no mind. Here, actions are unconscious. We no longer have to consciously think about a particular technique.

This is why habits are so hard to break, whether good habits or bad ones.

"You have to practice until you die."
Taisen Deshimaru, Japanese Buddhist teacher

Constant practice, constant firing and wiring of our brain, means we can perform effortlessly. This helps us to maintain our spirit.

Make a difference

When one of my students has been practising a particular technique, I immediately notice at the next lesson that they have improved. I will ask "Have you been practising?" and 90% of the time, they have! Usually only just for a minute or two, on one, two or three days. But the effect is significant.

Practising, just for three minutes a day, DOES make a difference.

How to practice

Practice does not make perfect. Practice makes permanent.

So when practising for something, such as a presentation, or a sport or a hobby, do it right. Do it for real. Practice as if you were in a real-life situation.

Every time we practice, we are educating and shaping our body and our mind that THIS is how it is done.

So when we need to use our skills, they are exactly what we need.

Practising is an ideal opportunity to explore something out of the heat of battle. If you can swim, the chances are that, if you had to, you could swim in the sea. Maybe even if the water was a bit choppy.

But you did not learn to swim in a choppy sea! You probably learnt in a swimming pool, in a safe secure environment, in clean, clear water.

And that is how it is with practising. Use practising as an opportunity to develop your skills, focusing on the particular technique or strategy that you wish to improve.

Black Belts practice regularly.

One Thing You Can DO Now:

Think of something you can practice, a skill you want to acquire or a strength you want to build on, and start practising now, for just three minutes.

Spirit

10 Introspection

"If introspection reveals the self to be unjust, then no matter how base the opponent may be, will I not be afraid? If introspection reveals the self to be just, then I will go, even though against a thousand or ten thousand men."
Gichin Funakoshi

Without being over obsessed with self, Black Belts are aware of their own thoughts and feelings.

When we match ourselves with what is going on around us, we can show great spirit and achieve extraordinary results, for ourselves and others.

Circle of Life

This is about being aware of exactly what is in our Circle of Life. It is about having courage and confidence, from knowing that we are operating from a position where we know and understand ourselves. We are consciously aware of who we are, what we are about to do, and the consequences of our actions.

We operate with thoughtfulness, never rashly or intending to cause harm.

Values

We have awareness of our values (see Awareness 5 Values) and our intended actions are congruent with our values. This gives us alignment, because we are matching what is important to us with the intended consequences of our actions.

So having done the introspection, we will go. Even against a thousand or ten thousand men.

This is the spirit of a Black Belt.

"I have cherished the ideal of a democratic and free society in which all persons live together in harmony and with equal opportunities. It is an ideal which I hope to live for and to achieve. But if needs be, it is an ideal for which I am prepared to die."
Nelson Mandela, 20th April 1964 in his defence against charges brought by the government of treason, sabotage and conspiracy.

Black Belts keep their spirit high by looking within, to check they are operating within their values, acting for the greater good.

One Thing You Can DO Now:

Think of a challenge you have in your life, and consider your own thoughts about this issue. Be clear that you are operating consciously, not intending harm, and take action now.

Spirit

You know the importance of spirit.
You know how to have the spirit of a Black Belt.

Humility

I Kara (empty)

As we discussed in Awareness 2 Self and Responsibility, the *Kara* in karate means empty. It means that all we have is empty hands, and that empty hands is all we need. Because we have ourselves.

But *Kara* has a deeper meaning, outside of the physical, a meaning that is the essence of this book.

Kara also means empty of self. Empty of ego.

> *"Just as it is the clear mirror that reflects without distortion, or the quiet valley that echoes a sound, so must one who would study karate-do purge himself of selfish and evil thoughts, for only with a clear mind and conscience can he understand that which he receives. This is another meaning of Kara in karate-do."*
> Gichin Funakoshi

Gichin Funakoshi described the ultimate aim of karate as the perfection of the character of its participants. When he was asked about this, he used one word.

Humility.

Grounded

The word humility comes from the word humus, which means grounded, from the earth.

When we think of people who show humility, they are grounded, they are in touch. In touch with themselves, how they think and feel, and in touch with others. They know that they are connected to something far larger than themselves.

Humility works

When empty of self, when we show humility, we can achieve extraordinary results:

- On June 5th 1989 in Tiananmen Square in Beijing, a man who was to become known as 'Tank Man' stopped the advance of a line of tanks. He was armed with two bags of shopping.

- Nelson Mandela and Mahatma Gandhi both overturned political regimes, peacefully, and established a sustainable democracy. Both demonstrated humility throughout their lives.
- Jose Mujica was the president of Uruguay from 2010 to 2015. On the day of his election he turned the presidential palace into a hostel for the homeless, and for five years he ran the country from his wife's farmhouse. Uruguay has outperformed neighbouring countries economically.
- In the book Good To Great by Jim Collins, leaders of the world's most successful companies, the truly great companies, had in common just two characteristics. They had a strong professional will; these people were very focused. And they had personal humility.
- Tony Hsieh founded online shoe retailer Zappos, and, with all the staff, embodied their philosophy in 10 Core Values. The tenth, and according to Tony Hsieh the most important value, was Be Humble. Zappos was sold for over $1 billion.

There are many more examples. Google's recruitment policy has five attributes, one of which is humility; the ability to step back from ownership of an idea if someone else's idea is better. And also intellectual humility, which means that their staff are willing to learn. (Only an empty or partially empty vessel can be filled, not one that thinks it is full.)

Humility and change
So politically and economically, humility delivers massive transformation. Humility delivers change that is sustainable, and amazing results.
Humility is when we make decisions and operate whilst being aware that we are part of something bigger than ourselves. We are not acting for OUR own interests, for our own goals and objectives, but for the greater good.

Humiliation?
At a karate lesson a few years ago several beginners turned up for

their first lesson. So I gave them my usual talk about the origins of karate, including a few words about humility.

At the end of the lesson I asked "What is the ultimate aim of the art of karate?"

One boy, very keen, shot his arm up and shouted "Humiliation".

Humility is almost the exact opposite of humiliation. As we shall explore in the next few sections, humility is about having high self-esteem, thinking well of ourselves AND others.

Black Belts know that karate is not about them. There is no place for their ego.

One Thing You Can DO Now:

Think of a challenge that you are facing, or something that you want to have. If you were to adopt a position of humility, where your ego was not involved, would that change things, and if so how?

2 Ego

Having an ego is the opposite of humility.

Ego is where someone focuses purely on self. They are full of self-importance, concerned only with their own vested interests, interests that serve them and them alone.

The problem with ego is that although it can appear strong, it is weak. Ego needs constant self-validation, constant reinforcement of THEIR interpretation of events. It needs constant energy to maintain itself. Whereas humility just is.

> Deri Llewellyn-Davies is a world-class speaker, author and adventurer. He has climbed the highest peaks on six continents, and has completed the Marathon des Sables, known as the MDS. The MDS is six marathons in seven days, carrying everything you need to survive on your back, through the Sahara Desert; it is known as the toughest foot race on earth.
>
> Deri tells how his ego got him to start the race, how he wanted to prove to himself and others that he could do it. But three days in to the race, he was struggling, and was in danger of falling behind the back marker, which would have meant being asked to stop the race. What got him through that phase, and to the finishing line, was humility. He realised it was not just about him. He did not have to be the best, some superhuman with no weaknesses or limitations. It was about being one part of a major experience, where he felt connected to everyone in his life; those around him, and those far away such as his family and friends.
>
> His ego got him to the start. His humility got him to the finish.

As well as extreme physical challenges there are other ways to achieve more humility in our lives. The rest of this section on humility gives us practical techniques and strategies that will enable us to put our ego to one side, if we so choose.

Indispensable?

The rationale behind ego does not hold true. People with high ego think they are indispensable. But a graveyard is full of indispensable people. They have died, and the earth continues to revolve, you and I continue to live, develop, have fun and do our stuff.

It is the people who have demonstrated humility who continue to have a place in our hearts and minds, whose actions continue to have an effect on our lives today.

Ego and posturing

When my *sensei*, Malcolm Phipps, demonstrates a fighting technique and asks someone to partner up with him, so that he can show the technique to the class, he always sinks DOWN into his stance.

Someone with ego would stand up, trying to be tall, to impose themselves on the other person. This is posturing. It looks good. It looks strong. But it is weak.

Someone standing up, as tall as they can be, looks strong and powerful. But they are vulnerable. Their throat is more exposed, and their legs are straight, meaning they are more inflexible, so they can't move as fast. And their groin, a key target area, is more exposed.

When we sink down, we present a smaller target. Our vulnerable areas are more covered. And our legs are flexed at the ankles and knees, so we can move faster, to attack or defend.

So if you ever have a confrontation with someone and they start by sinking DOWN, they have no ego. My advice is to run!

And our ego can get in the way. Our ego can make us seek perfection, when perhaps all we need to do is to do SOMETHING. To start, and perhaps achieve perfection later, or not seek it at all.

Somebody wants something

Here is a different approach to a situation, in business or perhaps in general life, where someone who you have a relationship with wants something. Something that might be at your expense, that might cause you some inconvenience if they were to have it.

Just give it to them. Just let them have it. Whatever it is that YOU want, put your ego to one side. For now, possibly for ever. Just give the other person what they are asking for.

I have used this tactic time and time again. It is one small concession that, as long as the status quo of the relationship is maintained, means you can just get on with more important things. And the relationship is enhanced. This is not to say that you always give way in negotiation, or that you let someone's ego develop out of control. But if these conditions do not apply, consider it as an option.

The humility of a beginner
In karate, a student attaining Black Belt can buy a silk Black Belt. Sometimes after their First Dan, or perhaps when they reach Second Dan. The black silk covers the white cotton underneath. Over many years, in fact decades, of training, the black silk wears away. Bits of black silk fray and drop off.

Over time, the student returns to being a white belt, to someone who has the humility of a beginner.

They know nothing, they know everything, they have gone full circle on their journey, and they start again.

They have no ego.

The people I follow, in life and business, do not ostentatiously display their knowledge or their skills. They are quiet humble men and women, a master of their trade, a specific skill or profession. From these people, we can learn much. Not just with regard to what they know, but also about humility.

"I have three precious things which I hold fast and prize. The first is gentleness; the second frugality; the third is humility, which keeps me from putting myself before others. Be gentle and you can be bold; be frugal and you can be liberal; avoid putting yourself before others and you can become a leader among men."
Lao-Tzu

"A true genius admits that he/she knows nothing."
Albert Einstein

Black Belts are on a life's journey to humility, a place where there is no ego, so that they can make a useful contribution to today's society.

One Thing You Can DO Now:

Think of a disagreement you may have had with someone recently. What would have happened if you had just let them have their way? Was it really THAT important that you had to get something out of it? What would your relationship with them look like now if you had, just that once, given them what they wanted?

3 Self-esteem

Self-esteem is how we feel about ourselves. It is how we see ourselves. It is our self-worth.
Having humility is about having HIGH self-esteem.

"All men (and women) are the same, except for their belief in their own selves, regardless of what others may think of them."
Miyamoto Musashi

When we have high self-esteem, our self-worth comes from within. High self-esteem is built up over many years. It is the rock, our foundation that cannot be shaken.

Value yourself

A top karate instructor was about to start a 90 minute karate course, when the parent of a child student on the course queried how much the course cost. He obviously thought it was too expensive for 90 minutes. The conversation went something like this:

"£30 for a 90 minute course?" (Parent)
"No, it's £30 for 35 years." (Instructor)
The parent handed the instructor £30 without further comment.

The instructor was referring to the skills and expertise that he had acquired through 35 years of training, some of it in Japan, some of it in England with world-class instructors.

Your value does not decrease because of someone's inability to see your worth. Monetary, or otherwise.
People pay us for our expertise that has taken years and sometimes decades to acquire. Not for their time that they deem to spend with us.
When we have high self-esteem, we know our value, we know how much we are worth, even if just in monetary terms. We put a price on it that reflects what we can do for others, the value that we bring to them.

Increasing our self-esteem

Here are some ways to increase our self-esteem. And to keep it high:

1) Be positive
2) Be forgiving of yourself
3) Be confident
4) See something good in everyone
5) Value others
6) Ask for help
7) Thank others

These are all covered in more detail throughout this book.

People with high self-esteem DO make mistakes. But they learn from them. They have the confidence to take risks, to learn new skills. They have a healthy attitude about their faults.

Black Belts have high self-esteem. They know they make mistakes, they are not perfect. They know their worth, in terms of money, love, friendship, support, empathy and everything that goes into making us the super human beings we are.

One Thing You Can DO Now:

Think of something you know you are good at. Is what you get back in return consistent with your estimation of what you are worth in providing this? (I am being deliberately vague here. It could be money, or it could an emotion in a particular relationship.)

4 Power

"Power is the ability to achieve purpose.
Power is the ability to effect change."
Martin Luther King, Jr.

People who demonstrate humility, in life, politics, and business, seem to have a special power.

"The less effort, the faster and more powerful you will be."
Bruce Lee

They are able to make massive changes with seemingly little effort.
Why is this?

Power or Force
It is because of the difference between power and force.
Force is about posturing, it is about show. Force needs energy to sustain it, just like ego. Force comes from ego.
Black Belts generally don't LOOK as if they are very strong. They don't have 'body builder' physiques, with massive muscles. If you look at their arms, their biceps are not particularly large. They don't have the classic 'Popeye' look.
But they can generate a lot of power.
The thing about muscles is that they only do one thing. Muscles contract. The biceps contract to bring the hand and forearm towards the shoulder and upper body. That is all they do.
So if you need to bring something heavy towards your upper torso, you will need big biceps.
But when we use our arms to punch or block, we need speed, not strength. And our arms need to go OUTWARDS, away from the body, not towards it. Black Belts have toned triceps, the muscles on the OPPOSITE side of the arm to the biceps. It is these we use to block and punch, because they act to straighten the arm, to take it away from the torso.
And so it is with generating power from humility. The source of the power is not always that obvious. What is most apparent, what is most visible, is

not what generates the power.

A man doing hard labour and in solitary confinement for 18 years on Robben Island had no obvious power. But Nelson Mandela changed the lives of 40 million people.

Achieving real power

To achieve power and demonstrate humility, there are some key concepts to be aware of:

People with humility take a long term view. They always see the bigger picture (see Chapter 9 in this section). They view setbacks as temporary and their personal situation as unimportant. When people apply force, which comes from their ego, they take a short term view, focusing only on what is directly in front of them.

People with humility are concerned with strategies, with how things are done, with processes. They know that this gives understanding and meaning, which are powerful. People operating from ego focus on tactics, which are short term and are the 'what' of what happens, not the 'why' or the 'how'.

People with humility just let things be, for now. They accept what is going on around them, and accept that the people caught up in doing 'bad' things are not necessarily themselves 'bad'. People operating from ego judge other people (see Humility 8 Judging Others).

People with humility usually choose to be assertive, stating how they feel and what they want to happen, without stating that it HAS to happen. People with ego who demonstrate force are aggressive. They bully, threaten or manipulate other people to get their own way. This is covered in Humility 7 Being assertive.

People with humility have awareness, the first main topic of this book. People operating from ego, who show force, have a narrow focus not seeing wider implications or the bigger picture.

Power	Force
Humility	Ego
Long term	Short term
Strategy	Tactics
Let be	Judge
Assertive	Aggressive
Awareness	Narrow focus

And as we have covered previously in this book, the journey towards the destination is so important. Military dictatorships aim to have what they call 'power'. It is power-based-on-force, where they want to rule and dominate others, not the true power we are covering here. But they always acquire it by force, which makes it unsustainable in the long term.

Black Belts don't apply force. They generate power and achieve extraordinary results by applying the subtle concepts of humility.

One Thing You Can DO Now:

If you have someone who is causing you problems in your life, take a concept that is based on power, not force. Take one concept from the table in this chapter and work out how to apply it to this situation.

5 Gratitude

People with humility are grateful. They are grateful for what they have, as opposed to wanting what they don't have.

Jose Mujica, the ex-President of Uruguay who demonstrated humility throughout his presidency, defines poverty as the gap between what you have and what you want. So even a 'rich' person can be poor, always wanting more, always needing to have that next thing.

Be grateful for what?

We have a lot to be grateful for. If you are reading this book, you have at least one eye that works, and probably two. You have the mental resources to be able to understand it (hopefully it IS making sense) and you had the financial resources to be able to buy it (unless you have stolen it!).

You have the spare time to read it, meaning you are not being held in slavery. You have access to outside resources and information, meaning you are not in bonded labour or living in a totalitarian regime. So you have a significant amount of freedom in your life, freedom to be able to do some of the things you want.

Isn't that a lot to be grateful for? There are 100s of millions of people around the world who do not have these freedoms.

Would you rather be you, with your life, or them?

Practising gratitude

I lived in Reading in Berkshire, UK and am a director with BNI, the world's largest networking organisation. Although most of our groups meet in the mornings, we hold a few events each year in the evening at a hotel. At some of these events we provide a light meal of chips and sandwiches.

I noticed that we were often having quite a bit of food left over. Food which one day I saw being thrown by the hotel staff into a clear plastic refuse sack. So I got in to the habit of taking the leftovers away with me, usually in a cardboard box, and walking around the centre of Reading until I found a homeless person I could give the box to.

One evening what really struck me, was that nearly every time I had done this, the response I got was that they would share the chips and sandwiches with other homeless people. They were grateful, and they then immediately thought of others. They were grateful for themselves AND their friends.

My one simple act, with one person, had a cascade effect and hopefully filled several empty stomachs on each particular night.

It is EASY to practice gratitude. Gratitude for ourselves, for what we do have, and for others. When we practice gratitude, it is human nature that we feel better about ourselves. It raises our self-esteem.

So be selfish. Be really, really selfish. Do something nice for someone else.

Gratitude in business networking

BNI has grown to be the world's largest networking organisation in my opinion because of two words.

Givers Gain™.

It starts with giving. The idea, proven many, many times around the world, is that those who give will gain.

Dr Ivan Misner founded BNI over 30 years ago. One of the many concepts he has covered in his books is the importance of showing gratitude to your referral sources.

Dr Misner says the two most effective ways of thanking your referral sources (people who give you referrals, introductions to future clients) is to send a hand-written card, and to meet up with them, to get to know their business and see if there is any way you can help them.

To keep this fresh in our minds, so that we are consciously AWARE of the importance of gratitude, remember the saying:

An attitude of gratitude

Black Belts know that practising gratitude increases their own self-esteem, so look for ways to be grateful. Grateful for their own situation, their own circumstances. And grateful to others.

One Thing You Can DO Now:

Give. Just give someone something. And notice how YOU feel.

6 Focus On Them

People with humility display amazing acts of gratitude and thoughtfulness for others.

"Humility is not thinking less of yourself, it is thinking of yourself less."
C.S. Lewis (novelist and poet)

When we think of ourselves less, we have more time to think of others, to focus on them. What they want. How they think and feel.

> Before he retired my father was a Chief Executive in the NHS, responsible for several hospitals and 6,000 staff. One day my brother finished work and went to meet him in his office, in a hospital in Lancaster.
> As they were walking along the corridor towards the exit, my father went up to one of the cleaners who was polishing the floor, one of the 6,000 staff he was responsible for. And he said "Hello Mary, how is your son?"
> He knew her name, he knew her son had been ill, and he was enquiring after his well-being.

Top leaders, people who inspire others, focus on other people. Not in a planned, calculating way. But because they care.
In all areas of our lives, we have the opportunity to demonstrate humility by focusing and enquiring after other people. To support them when they need it, if we are able to give it. To make a difference. Not for our sake, but for theirs.

Be a networking ninja
When people are networking, they often ask for an introduction to a dream client. It is all too easy to focus on why it is so good for that person to be introduced to their dream client. Well, good for them!
You can be different. You can be a networking *ninja*.
Instead, focus on why this dream client would want to speak to you.
This requires a bit of thought on your part. But if YOU don't do this thinking,

this crucial part of the process, no-one else will. And all too often it just doesn't happen, and people's requests, requests that could transform their business, are not answered.

If I were to get you an introduction to a dream client, I only really need to know two things. Who you want to speak to, and what I will say to them. And that's it.

Knowing what is in it for them, because you have focused on them, makes the second part easy.

And if you want an introduction to a referral partner, someone who could provide you with an ongoing stream of referrals, you have to be clear about what is in it for THEM as well as their (and hopefully your) clients. And it probably won't be to do with money.

So be a networking *ninja*, and focus on what is in it for them.

This concept applies to all areas of business. Want to develop a killer value proposition? Focus on your existing and future customers.

Want to be a top speaker? Focus on the value you will deliver to the audience.

Want to be a top salesperson? Focus on how your products or services will help your prospect.

Black Belts know how to look after their own self-esteem, so they are not too concerned about themselves. This means there is space in their lives for others. Black Belts help and support other people.

One Thing You Can DO Now:

Think of something you want, something you want from someone. What do they want? Put yourself in their shoes, work out what THEY want, and help them get it. The chances are that you will get what you want too.

7 Being Assertive

Being assertive is the middle ground between being passive and being aggressive.

Being in the middle of these two extremes is where we find balance, the balanced view of reason and stability.

Aggressive

People who are aggressive are operating from ego. They tend to dominate, they threaten and abuse. They can be violent.

Some of this aggression is to mask weaknesses. In fact, aggressive people ARE weak.

Let's say someone grabs your throat. This is pretty aggressive! It is strong.

But let's think about it. You both have two hands. One of their hands is out of action, perhaps just for a second or two, but for right now, it is busy.

You have two hands and both are free. You might only have a second to act (and you would need to think about your Awareness, about how you got in to this position, but that can wait until later). And because they are within touching/grabbing distance of you, you are within touching distance of them!

You have many options. You can control their hand/arm round your throat (although you would need to know one or two techniques to do this). You can focus on being ready to block an attack from their other arm. You can just attack them, with either hand, to the eyes, throat or other vital areas. You can kick them or knee them in the groin. You can sweep them (unbalance them with your leg). You might be able to shout for help. You might be able to bite their grabbing forearm or hand. (They have attacked first, unprovoked, so morally and legally you can take REASONABLE action.)

There are many things you can do, which before they grabbed you, you could not. They have more weaknesses.

When we are attacked physically, or feel attacked emotionally, the key thing to remember is that we have options because the other person has weaknesses.

Acting assertively

Although people who are passive do not express their feelings or say what they WANT to happen, people who are assertive do. People who are assertive:

- Say what they think and how they feel
- Focus on the self-esteem of everyone
- Are firm and polite
- Respect the rights of others, including THEIR right to be assertive
- Aim for a Win-Win scenario every time

How to be assertive

Maintaining our self-esteem and acting from humility will help us to be assertive, rather than passive or even aggressive.

In a verbal exchange with someone who is being aggressive, there is a simple technique to follow where you can be assertive:

1 Show that you have listened and understand what they are saying
2 Say 'however' or 'and' (not 'but', this is too confrontational)
3 Say what you think and how you feel
4 Say what you want to happen now

And if you get resistance to this, one option is to play the 'broken record', repeating these points.

Black Belts are assertive, never aggressive, always aware of what they want for themselves and what other people want.

One Thing You Can DO Now:

Think of a conflict situation, or where in a relationship with someone, something does not feel quite right. Let the other person know how you feel and state what you want to happen, and let them

do the same. Then see if you can work to an amicable solution, where you both get some or all of what you both want.

8 Judging Others

"If you judge people, you have no time to love them."
Mother Teresa

People with humility are aware that they are not perfect, and neither is anyone else.
Accepting imperfections, in ourselves and others, is necessary for us all to live together.

"The mountain does not laugh at the river because it is lowly
And the river does not laugh at the mountain because it cannot move."
The Little Book of Seishinkai

Labels
If we were to judge others for their imperfections, we would be giving them a label. This would be a very slippery slope!
How long would it be before we started giving certain groups of people certain types of label? We are then on the way to developing an 'ism'. For example sexism, where men, or women, have certain types of faults, just because they are a man, or a woman. Or racism. Or ageism, where people are discriminated against on the basis that they are a certain age.
Judging others means that we do not have to think. Because when we judge, we are just reinforcing our beliefs. We are helping to validate our beliefs, whether they are true or not.
Judging means we do not have to focus on them. Because they are a man, or woman, or this race, or that age, then they are likely to have these faults. (Judging is rarely about strengths or positive qualities.)
But when we investigate further, we find exceptions. When we get to know people, then these stereotypes generally do not hold true. We find there are far more exceptions than not!

Weaknesses and strengths
People who have humility know that we all have our weaknesses, and we all have our strengths. We are all different. Every single one of us is good at some things, our strengths, and less good at others, our weaknesses.

So one way for us to enhance our humility is to be aware of ourselves if we were to inadvertently judge other people. Be aware of making stereotypes and giving people labels.

When we judge people, we are divisive. We are making a barrier between them and us. We are preventing us from feeling connected to other people, so it is working against us.

Others judging us

A well-documented psychological phenomenon is the Spotlight effect, where people believe they are in the spotlight. They believe that everyone else is noticing them, as if they are the actor on a stage.

In a famous study, students were asked to enter a room wearing a T-shirt with a picture of Barry Manilow. (Students and Barry Manilow don't really go together.) They were then asked how many of the other students in the room had noticed them wearing the embarrassing T-shirt.

The students over-estimated how many of their colleagues had noticed their T-shirt, by 100%! Only a quarter had noticed their T-shirt, but the T-shirt wearers thought that half had noticed.

This shows that we over-estimate the extent to which other people notice us and judge us. Most of the time most people don't even notice us!

What other people think of me is none of my business

If you feel that other people are judging you it is necessary to take some (mental) action, to safeguard your self-esteem, to keep you at humility. A very powerful phrase to remember, which I have shared with teenagers who have felt it really helped, is:

> "The people that judge don't matter
> Because the people that matter don't judge."

If someone is judging you, do they really matter? Are they massively important in your life? Probably not.

Black Belts don't judge. They expect everyone to give THEIR best, whatever that may be, and they respect everyone, regardless of sex, race, religion, age or anything else.

One Thing You Can DO Now:

If you feel someone is judging YOU, ask yourself if they really matter to you in your life? Yes, they are entitled to their opinion, just as you are entitled to ignore it.

9 Bigger Picture

One way to move towards humility is to see the bigger picture.
Everything we do, think and feel is just one part of a larger entity. We are one person out of over seven billion on this planet.

Belonging

By focusing on the larger entity, we focus less on our self. We develop a sense of belonging, as we realise we are a part of something outside of ourselves. By feeling that we belong to something bigger than us, we realise that we share common values with others.

We are never truly alone. We share common values, hopes and aspirations with all sorts of different people. People from different backgrounds, different races, different religions. There are bonds we cannot see, connections that we are not consciously aware of.

For some people, this is their religious journey. They realise that they are part of something that has other dimensions, other powers that they can be part of. Whether religious or not, realising we are part of something bigger than us helps us keep things in perspective. This is why people with humility are not unduly troubled by problems and setbacks. When viewed against the bigger picture, these are much less significant.

Overcoming obstacles

There are always obstacles and hurdles to overcome.
I know several Black Belts who have 'failed' a grading. I have 'failed' two. My instructor, Malcolm Phipps, 'failed' his Second Dan grading exam, when the members of his newly-formed association were watching him!
He was focused on developing a karate association that followed the traditional approach of the JKA (Japan Karate Association).
He is now an 8th Dan Black Belt and runs a worldwide karate association. Nelson Mandela was kept a prisoner on Robben Island for 18 years, and was imprisoned for a total of 27 years. Jose Mujica was imprisoned for 13 years during the military dictatorship in Uruguay.
They played the long game, and kept their values and their identity intact. 13 years is a significant amount of time in a life's journey.

So when we look at our way, our journey, in totality, we are more stable. The short-term ups and downs, that are a part of all our lives, are put in to their proper significance.

Yes, setbacks are frustrating, and life has its fair share of disappointments. When viewed against the overall journey, these are mere blips on a long, rewarding journey.

Comfort Zone

When we feel we belong to something bigger than ourselves, we feel there is a connection between us and 'it'. That we are part of it and it is part of us.

We feel at one. At one with everything. Because we are one and the same. Developing the concept of our Comfort Zone (which we covered in Awareness 7 Circle of Life), we become comfortable everywhere. Everything is us, we are everything.

We effectively have no boundaries or barriers. Everything is already a part of who we are.

The big picture in business

Quite often in business, if a competitor drops their prices, the other company feels they have to drop THEIR prices. But when we consider the bigger picture, we see that this is just one option. There are many others! The first option is always to do nothing. This is the option against which all other options must be evaluated.

Other options include RAISING prices, dropping them slightly, dropping them a lot, keeping prices the same and focusing more on marketing, announcing a new product or service. There are many options, which we can see clearly when we view the picture overall, rather than a knee-jerk short-term reaction.

We are more creative when we see the bigger picture.

Networking tip

When people go networking, the cardinal sin is to sell to the room.

One reason people do this is because they only see the people in the room. They are not seeing the bigger picture. It is said that every person knows about 1,000 people. That means that if you are at a networking event where there are 30 people, there are 30,000 people who you could get an introduction to. Just from the people in the room!

So don't sell TO the room. Sell THROUGH the room, by building relationships based on trust with the people in front of you.

Black Belts know that by viewing the big picture, short-term problems will be less significant, meaning they are less stressed and better placed to overcome the problem they are currently facing.

One Thing You Can DO Now:

Think of a problem or setback you may have had recently, or think you are about to have. Take a long term view, and consider just how important this really is.

10 KISS (Keep It Simple Sweetheart)

*"The balance between victory and defeat often
hangs on simple matters."*
Gichin Funakoshi

Making things complicated is ego. Keeping things simple is humility.

"Only a great spirit dares to have a simple style."
Anon, from *The Little Book of Seishinkai*

It is ego that makes people complicate things. So that they can appear the expert, or perhaps so that they can have some control over the information or process. And they can continue to develop their idea, making it more complicated. Perhaps inventing work for themselves.

In Awareness 9 Risk I told the story of how the doorman had faced and overcome two knife attacks. He had previously been taught a very complicated defence system for knife attacks.
Just before the two incidents where he faced real-life attacks, he had also been taught a very simple system, based on GUN (Grab, Undo, Neutralise). It was the GUN system that he used both times. It was simple, so it was easy to remember, and it was effective.
One of the secrets behind Apple's success is that Steve Jobs had an obsession with keeping things simple. He used to 'hit' people with his Simple Stick if he felt an idea or concept could be further distilled down to its core components.

Complicated doesn't work
As we covered in Spirit 1 Spirit or Technique, in a fight many techniques, especially kicks, won't work.
It is the complicated kicks that won't work, like the reverse spinning roundhouse kick. This kick even sounds complicated.
But the simple kicks, that directly attack the groin or lower abdomen, will work.
The kicks you see in movies are there to look good. They are complicated

to perform. They take time and effort to deliver.

A fight scene in a movie where there was a direct, good attack to the groin would be a very short fight scene!

Hard or easy

Just keeping things simple does not mean they will be easy. Top karate instructors say that karate is simple, but it is also hard.

I have heard this said about many other things, in business and in life. Keeping things simple is not a lazy short-cut. Sometimes a lot of effort goes in to keeping things simple.

But when we keep things simple, communication is clearer. Everyone knows where they stand. It is easier to benchmark success, to know exactly what is effective. It is easy to keep track of any improvements or modifications.

Black Belts keep things as simple as they can, because this is the best guarantee that they will work if required.

One Thing You Can DO Now:

Think of a problem or challenge you are facing. WHAT exactly is the problem? Distil it down to its core essence. Make the issue a simple one, where you have one thing to focus on. Keep it simple.

You know the importance of humility.
You know how to have the humility of a Black Belt.

Decision

I Perfect Time

All the theories and strategies in the world are worth nothing unless there is action. Until somebody does something. And there will not be action until a decision is made. Next we look at what stops us making decisions, and how we can make faster and better decisions, so that we take decisive action.

Not NOW

It is easy not to do something in the belief that NOW is not the perfect time. Or even a good time.

So perhaps at some undefined point in the future, there will be a better time.
A time when you are more prepared for the consequences of the action.
A time when circumstances will be more favourable.
A time when perhaps you can rely more on other people.
A time when you have learned that extra golden nugget that means that this time you WILL succeed, and the act will be easy to do.
A time when everything else is in place, so that this one simple act will have massive, favourable, consequences.
There will never be this time.

When is the perfect time?

There is never the perfect time. Consider this:

> If you were to attack me, there COULD be a perfect time.
> It would be a time when I was standing directly in front of you. I would have my eyes closed, so I wouldn't be able to see you. My hands would be behind me, trapped between my belt and my karate suit, so I couldn't easily free them to be able to use them to block your attack. My legs would be straight and spread apart, so I would be unable to move quickly and would be exposing vulnerable areas.
> You would attack and you would win.

I am not going to do this.

There will never be this time.

Just attack me, I'll defend, I'll then attack you (not at a perfect time), you will block, and so on. We will both over time develop our fighting skills.

Black Belts know there is never a perfect time to do anything. When they feel reasonably comfortable, they just decide to go, they just take action.

One Thing You Can DO Now:

Think of something you have been putting off. Accept there is no perfect time, so decide NOW to just go and do it.

2 Perfection

One of the barriers to making a decision is aiming for perfection.

Perfection and outer space

The Hubble Telescope is one of the largest space telescopes ever made. It was launched in 1990 and is estimated to have cost $2.5 billion to build. Just a few weeks after having been launched, it was noticed that some of the images it was producing were a bit fuzzy!

The telescope was not focusing. The problem was the 2.4 metre mirror was wrong, it was not perfect.

It was out by two thousandths of a millimetre. Two thousandths (0.002) of a millimetre, out of 2,400.000 millimetres. That is an accuracy of 99.99991%.

Good enough for most things, but not for seeing into the darkest reaches of the universe.

Even something costing $2.5 billion was not perfect.

Ego

It is often our ego that means that we aim for perfection (unless we are building state-of-the-art space telescopes). We need to look good in front of others, and to validate our own fragile self-worth.

People with humility do not need to be assured of perfection. They just decide to start.

In 2014 I was very ill on two occasions. I was an emergency admission to hospital twice in six months. It took me a while to recover from the second illness.

Once I had got my health back, I started to get fitter, and to do some gentle karate at home. I was teaching at my club, but I needed to train.

I didn't feel the time was quite right to start training. I would be far from perfect.

As soon as I realised I was hoping for perfection, that I was wishing I would immediately return to my previous level (which admittedly is far from perfect!), I went and trained.

I was not perfect. I was not that good to be honest.

But I was back.

Aiming for perfection can be a good thing. But it can be a reason never to start. To procrastinate indefinitely.

My instructor knew I had been ill. He could see that I was not that good. But he was glad, as I was, that I had come back and trained.

And this will be the case in life. People will cut you some slack. They know reality and perfection very rarely go together. They will often give you some credit just for having a go. Whether you are perfect or not.

Their perfection?

One person's perfection can be another person's imperfection.

This state of 'perfection' that we aim for, might just be our state, our opinion. Our perfection might be solely something that WE think of as being perfect. Something that is subjective.

But even if we reach it, others, justifiably from their point of view, may see it as something else. Apart from mathematical numbers, there is no one absolute state of 'perfection.' So this state of perfection does not exist! There is no point in aiming for it.

Things change

As we progress and develop, things change.

When a beginner in karate starts doing a front snap kick, we emphasise the importance of bringing the knee up first.

Just as with Keith (Spirit 4 Limiting Beliefs), it is important for the knee to come up first, so that the kicking foot extends outwards horizontally. Black Belts don't kick like that. There is less focus on the knee, and more focus on the foot going in a straight line from where it is on the floor, to its destination. But all the other body parts, such as the supporting foot, the hips, and the torso, move AS IF the knee has come up.

So the technique changes as the student moves up through the karate grades.

What was initially a 'perfect' technique for a beginner would be a poor technique for a Black Belt.

The technique changes as the student progresses.

This is what happens in life. In business and in our personal life, what was 'good', 'perfect', becomes less so.

And we have to adapt to improve. So even if we had somehow managed to achieve 'perfect' there would just become another 'perfect' to attain.

So don't bother with perfect. Just decide to start.

Black Belts don't aim for perfection, they just decide to get stuck in, to have a go. Getting anywhere close to 'perfection' is something that may happen later, or it may not. The key thing is to start.

One Thing You Can DO Now:

Is there you have something you have been putting off? Something that you want to be perfect, but are not sure how to make it perfect? Go and do it. Or at least decide now, actually put something in your diary, that you WILL start. It won't be perfect, at least not straight away. But you can make the decision NOW to do it.

Decision

3 Kaizen

Kaizen is the concept of continuous improvement.

It is a concept that has been well used in the business world, and is thought to be behind the meteoric rise of Japan's economy in the second half of the 20th century. It is a good solution to the problem of aiming for perfection. Because if we accept that we will continually improve, we accept that things NOW are not perfect. We will aim for perfection, but right NOW things are not perfect, so we will continually improve.

Change

'*Kai*' means change, and '*zen*' means good. So *kaizen* means change for good, change for the better.

We know that the one constant thing, in business and in life, is change. With some changes, we can continue as we are. But with some changes, we ourselves then need to make changes. Changes to adapt, because the playing field has altered.

Kaizen is about small steps. Making small but distinct changes, to improve or progress towards a goal or objective.

One thing at a time

The way that karate was traditionally taught in Japan was to have a lesson where there was a particular theme, just for that lesson.

The theme could be use of the hips, or the uninvolved arm, or breathing, or any one of many components of a technique.

By isolating this one theme, it could be worked on in all the various moves and techniques. There would be improvements across all areas of the students' karate – in basics, blocking, stances and every other aspect. Just by focusing on one thing.

And the next lesson would have another theme.

Black Belts embrace the concept of kaizen, accepting that they are never perfect and change happens all the time. They take one thing, work on it, improve it, and then focus on something else.

One Thing You Can DO Now:

Facing a big challenge? Take just one aspect, and put all your energy into that one aspect. Forget all the other components, just focus on that one thing, and make it better.

Decision

4 Certainty

When Black Belts have made a decision to act, they act with certainty.
They have the firm conviction that what they intend to happen WILL
happen. There are no doubts.

Acting with certainty gives us confidence.

Certainty and selling

When selling services, or in the case of seeking a job then selling us,
ourselves, there are two things that the 'buyer' needs. In fact they crave
them.

The second most important thing is value for money. Perceiving that they
have got a 'good deal'. The best possible deal to get.

But the most important thing is certainty.

There is no point in buying a car or a loaf of bread that represents the best
value for money, if the car has major engine failure the first time you drive
it, or if the bread is stale.

People, 'buyers', crave certainty. Especially in a recession, when times
are hard.

Convincing with certainty

The way to convince people that something will do what you are saying it
will, is to prove you have done it before.

Let's say I wanted to convince you, sell you the idea, that I could run 100
metres in less than 10 seconds. That is world athlete class (and I'm not
an athlete, let alone a world class one).

I could tell you my training regime, how I looked after my diet, the
proficiency of my training partners, the books I had read and the research
I had undertaken. And you still probably wouldn't believe me.

But if I were to tell you that last week I ran 100 metres in 9.9 seconds, you
may well change your opinion.

The certainty of having already done something is a very powerful
convincing strategy.

This is why in BNI, and in business life generally, testimonials are so
powerful. They help to convince the people reading and hearing the

testimonial that this person can do this!

Black Belts know that acting with certainty, and BELIEVING in certainty, gives them confidence and power.

One Thing You Can DO Now:

If you are 'selling' something, focus on how you can increase the certainty that what you are 'selling' will do what you say it will.

Decision

5 Moving Forwards

When we decide to act, we move forwards, literally or metaphorically. Black Belts know that there are only three possible ways to move forwards.

Oi Ashi   **To step forwards**

> With one leg in front of the other, this is where we move the back leg up so that it is level with the front leg and then onwards to the front. This is what we do when we walk and run. With a slightly longer stance, a karate stance, this is how we do a full on attack.

This is full commitment towards a big goal. We are moving forwards, directly towards our goal (in karate, usually the other person!).There is no subtlety here, we are acting decisively, marching towards what we have decided we want, where we need full commitment.

This could be deciding to ask for a raise, or to contact that big prospective client to find if they want to go ahead with our services. We just go and do it. We take one decisive action.

Suri Ashi   **To half step forwards**

> With one leg in front of the other, this is where we move the back leg halfway to the front leg, we just do a half step. We then step forwards with the FRONT leg, reaching further than we could just a few moments ago.

This is where we need to prepare, to make the decisive act more effective. We WILL do one critical move, but we need to get things ready first. So that when we do move, it is with conviction, enabling us to reach further and achieve more than we could have done previously.

This could be deciding to change our job, where we need to stop procrastinating, get our CV up-to-date, contact firms and/or recruitment companies, let our contacts know we are looking, practice our interview technique, prepare for the type of questions will be asked etc. And then we are ready for interviews, with the right companies, fully prepared.

Yori Ashi   **To slide step forwards**

> The front leg moves forwards. The back leg WILL follow (I have never seen it get left behind, becoming somehow unattached to the rest of the person's body).

This is where we realise that we can get something quick, that we just have to act. So we just do it. There is no preparation.
This could be asking for a date, or putting your prices up.

Black Belts know they have three options to get what they want, and are aware of the merits of each strategy.

One Thing You Can DO Now:

Think of something you want and plan your strategy on how you are going to get it.
Will you get it by demonstrating full commitment, acting decisively (Oi Ashi)?

Will you get it by preparing first, getting everything ready (Suri Ashi)?

Will you get it by just doing it, realising that it is probably within your grasp (Yori Ashi)?

Decision

6 Motivation

If you want to be a Black Belt in karate, there are only two things you need. Firstly, you need someone at the front, the instructor or *sensei*, who knows what they are talking about. They have to know what they are doing, in terms of the art of karate, and in terms of being able to pass on what they have learnt. They are able to teach effectively. And they have to keep the discipline in the class, to minimise accidents, and make sure the time is spent on learning and doing karate. And to be able to notice if a student is not giving 100%, and know what to do if they are not.

And the other thing is, you need to want it.

This is like life.

To succeed, in any aspect of life, you have to want to succeed. Very few things, things that are really worth having, or problems in our life that we would like to resolve, will just happen of their own accord. You have to make it happen, and to do that, you have to be motivated to do it, to want to do it.

But HOW do we want things? And how can we manage the extent to which we do, or don't, want them?

Managing our motivation is a crucial component of managing our success.

Internal, external

In Awareness 2 Self and Responsibility we explored Locus of Control, the degree to which we internalise or externalise ideas, concepts, responsibility and many other things.

The same is true with motivation, how we motivate ourselves.

Motivation is either intrinsic (internalised) or extrinsic (externalised).

With intrinsic motivation we are doing something for our OWN sake, our own feelings and self-esteem. Intrinsic motivation is concerned with self. We want to achieve or solve something because we are interested in doing so for us.

Someone motivated by extrinsic factors is concerned with the recognition and thoughts of others, of what will happen OUTSIDE of themselves, after the goal has been reached or the problem has been solved.

Intrinsic (internalised) motivation is the stronger of the two. Intrinsic motivators are more powerful than extrinsic motivators. Intrinsic motivators are more aligned with humility, whereas extrinsic motivators are more aligned with ego.

> The Harry Potter actor who got his Black Belt never trained again (as we covered in Strategy 3 Goals). Why? Because he wanted his Black Belt for his acting career, to be able to show to OTHERS that he was a Black Belt. This is extrinsic motivation.
> It worked. He did get what he wanted. But as soon as he had got what he wanted, that was it. He stopped. Permanently.

To, Away

Another concept we can use to manage our motivation is to know whether we are motivated by going To, or Away From something.

If we are motivated by going To, then we are looking ahead, focusing on having success, pleasure, triumph, winning.

If we are motivated by going Away, then we are focusing on avoiding, not having, failure, pain, defeat or loss.

And fear can motivate us. But remember, FEAR stands for False Expectations Appearing Real. Fears, just like beliefs, are not reality.

Being motivated To something, or Away from something, works. It is just knowing, being aware, of what motivates us best.

Other theories

There are many other ways to be able to achieve the right level of motivation, including Maslow's Hierarchy of Needs and Herzberg's Motivation-Hygiene theory. If neither of the two methods described above work for you, try another method to manage your level of motivation.

Black Belts, the Black Belts who keep training AFTER they have reached their first Black Belt, are motivated by intrinsic factors, they are doing it for them. This does not it mean it is selfish, they may wish to reach a high level so that they can motivate and inspire others and get them to a high level.

Decision

One Thing You Can DO Now:

Think of something you want. Why do you want it? Is it for yourself, or is it for something that you will then get from other people? If other people are involved, then your motivation is extrinsic and might be weak, so focus on the intrinsic reasons, the reasons why YOU want it.

7 *Discipline*

Black Belts have two types of discipline.

Group
The first type of discipline is the group discipline of karate, which applies to everyone in the *dojo*.

This is where things are done in a certain way, and in karate it starts with everyone bowing as they enter and leave the *dojo*. It also includes the discipline of staying still if we are not doing a technique. It means we stop immediately when told to stop (see Acceptance 3 *Yame*).

Group discipline is external discipline. It is a discipline that has originated from outside of the self, and is imposed on the practitioners. This type of discipline is common to all traditional martial arts.

This type of discipline also helps to minimise accidents. It means we don't mess around, that we take things seriously. It means we are all acting as one, and no one person can disrupt the class.

Personal
The other type of discipline is our own discipline. It is the discipline we have to train, to train hard, always giving it our 100%, whatever that may be at the time. It is the discipline that makes us turn up if we feel a bit ill. The discipline to practice, whether we feel like it or not.

This is self-discipline. It comes from within.

It is the self-discipline to do the 'extra' bits that makes the difference.

Since 1/1/91 I have had the discipline to keep a karate diary, which was suggested by my instructor.

In the lesson on 2nd January 1991, we practiced four elbow techniques. In January 1991 I also trained on the 5th, 7th, 10th, 12th, 14th, 16th, 18th, 21st, 24th and 28th.

Every technique, everything I learned at each lesson since 1/1/91, is in my diary. I wrote up each lesson at home each night, even if it was 10pm on a Wednesday night and I was tired from training.

I am now on my third volume of my karate diary.

My karate diary is the single most important resource I have for my karate.

Decision

It is about me. It is my experiences, what I have done, what I have learned. It has been invaluable in planning lessons as an instructor, especially once there were Black Belts in the class and I was teaching advanced techniques, combinations and strategies.

What would your diary be?

How do you record what you have learned?

How would you have the discipline to maintain it?

Black Belts take the stress out of making many decisions, because they have high self-discipline. There is no decision to make. Discipline has already decided that they are going to do it, whether it is as simple as keeping a diary, or something very complicated.

One Thing You Can DO Now:

Think of a resource you would like to have, or a skill you would like to develop, something that requires a 'little and often' in terms of effort. Just decide now that you will do something small, and often, and decide that you will have the discipline to do it. Every time.

8 Trust

Martial arts done well are reasonably safe. There is SOME risk, just as there is a risk in crossing the road or playing a sport or walking down stairs. Trust helps to minimise risk.

Having trust means that we can more easily make decisions and take action, because we have minimised risk, the risk of something going wrong.

Self-trust

The most important type of trust is to trust ourselves.

Trust of ourselves comes from knowing and accepting ourselves. We can raise our trust by keeping the promises we make, to ourselves and others. Be aware of your self-talk. Remember this comes from limiting beliefs, but a Black Belt can defeat the *ninjas* of negative self-talk (see Spirit 5 Self-talk). Keep your self-talk positive.

When we completely trust ourselves, we have no doubts, and increased confidence. It is easier to make decisions, to act decisively.

Trust takes time

Trusting others, and getting other people to trust us, takes time.

In karate, after a few lessons a beginner starts doing some gentle 'fixed' sparring.

They do a nominated attack to their partner, and then hold their position, they freeze. This is so that their partner, having practiced a 'live' block, can also practice and work on their counter. Practice the counter attack in terms of where they aim it, and the distance to wherever they are aiming. Over time, these counter attacks, to a stationary target, get closer and closer to touching the initial attacker.

Black Belts get very close, in fact we intend to touch the target area. Often we punch each other in the throat (do NOT try this at home), using the high degree of control we have built up through our training. This means we know the technique will be effective, whoever has attacked us.

This really does take trust. Trust that has been built up over months and years of training together.

The golden rule is that trust takes time.

According to the psychologist Robert Zajonc, we treat new things with caution, because as human beings we are hard-wired for survival. When we have experienced things a few times, we start to trust them, to feel safe.

Trust in networking
When I deliver networking talks, using the knowledge I have learned with BNI I explain how we need to take small steps on the road to trust with a new person we meet at a networking event.

One of the things I recommend is that, to build trust with someone who you have only just met, you promise to do one thing after the meeting. It may be to email them some useful information. Or to connect with them on LinkedIn. Or to put them in touch with a contact who could be useful for them.

Just one simple thing to do, that takes just one or two minutes.

And then do it.

This starts a solid relationship, as it already has some element of trust.

Black Belts know that trust takes time. Trust of ourselves, trust of others, and of others trusting us.

One Thing You Can DO Now:

Make a promise to yourself that you will do something in the future. And make sure you do it!

9 Commitment

Commitment is getting involved with something at a deep level.
Commitment goes hand in hand with high self-esteem.
People with low self-esteem tend to have the belief that they have nothing
to contribute. So it is not worth them making a contribution, to them getting
involved. Their involvement won't make much difference, they don't have a
significant part to play. They won't really commit to anything.
People with high self-esteem tend to believe that they DO have something
to contribute. And what they do will make a difference. They DO commit.

Committing gives power

The strongest kick in karate is *Ushiro geri*, reverse kick. The kicker pivots
360 degrees, to build up speed and make full use of the hips.
Ushiro geri is rarely seen in competition, because of the extra time it takes
to rotate the body 360 degrees. It is not a fast, snap kick. It is a thrust kick,
generating a lot of power.
It is the commitment, the commitment of the whole body, that gives the
kick its power.

Commitment has a power of its own.

"Until one is committed, there is hesitancy, the chance to draw back,
always ineffectiveness. Concerning all acts of initiative (and creation),
there is one elementary truth that ignorance of which kills countless
ideas and splendid plans: that the moment one definitely commits
oneself, then Providence moves too. All sorts of things occur to help
one that would never otherwise have occurred. A whole stream of
events issues from the decision, raising in one's favour all manner of
unforeseen incidents and meetings and material assistance, which no
man could have dreamed would have come his way."
WH Murray (Scottish mountaineer and writer)

When we commit, doubts are removed. We have more confidence.
When we commit to something, we have more power.
So we achieve more, with the same amount of effort.

Decision

Don't 'try'

Committing is about starting something certain in the knowledge that you are going to do it.

> *"Try not. Do, or do not. There is no try."*
> Yoda (*Star Wars*)

Committing is a mental state, where it just IS. It IS going to happen, the future is now. It is almost as if it has already happened, and you are running through history. You are not trying to do it. It is as if it has been done.

Test the commitment of others

A useful technique to see how interested other people are, is to test their commitment.

In business, say you have a prospect that you are unsure of. Are they a real prospect, or have they just been kidding you along? Test their commitment by asking for a meeting with them. If they are happy to commit their time, then they are genuinely interested. If they are not willing to commit their time, they are not committed to going ahead.

> *"Whatever you can do, or dream you can do, begin it.*
> *Boldness has genius, power, and magic in it. Begin it now."*
> Johann Wolfgang von Goethe

Black Belts either do something with full commitment, or they don't do it. This means they operate free of doubts, full of confidence, generating massive power.

One Thing You Can DO Now:

Think of something that you want. Maybe something to do with a relationship. Or perhaps your business life, where you would like to grow your business, or develop your career. And give an honest answer to the question "Am I interested in growing my business, or am I COMMITTED to growing my business"? Decide which you are, and then think about how you feel.

10 Do It

Sometimes, even when someone is ready to DO something, they continue to plan. Avoiding taking action, avoiding actually doing something, just tweaking and refining their plan.

Planning and change

Making plans is great. It means we are prepared, and have given thought to what we are about to do. We are more likely to be successful than if we didn't plan.

But we can over-plan, and rely on the plan itself to carry us through to the end destination.

But change happens. The environment changes, WE change, other people don't do what we expected.

A better strategy may include the importance of *zanshin*, being aware of ourselves, others and the external environment. So that we can make changes quickly, deviating from the original plan, but still focused on our 'way'.

So that we accept that we will never to be able to predict everything that will happen, that the plan is good enough to start, so we may as well just do it now.

Right, wrong, no

There are only three possibilities regarding making a decision:

We have made the right decision
We have made the wrong decision
We make no decision.

If we make the right decision, happy days! If we make the wrong decision, things can still turn out right, and we can learn and progress.

Making NO decision, not acting, is the worst. Nothing gets done! There is no opportunity to achieve something for ourselves, or to help other people, or to learn from our mistakes.

Decision

"If you spend too much time thinking about a thing,
you'll never get it done."
Bruce Lee

Easy decisions

Make it easy to make decisions, to do things.

Barack Obama only wears blue or grey suits. So when he has to decide which colour of suit to wear each day, it is a very straight-forward 'either/ or' decision. It is blue, or grey.

This enables him to save the mental powers required for making decisions for later in the day, when he needs to make more important decisions!

Black Belts know when the plan is 'good enough', and then take action, they just do it.

One Thing You Can DO Now:

Think of a decision that you would like to make, so that you take some action. What can you do to make the process of making decisions easier for you? So that you just DO IT?

You know the importance of making a decision to do something.
You make decisions like a Black Belt.

Part Two
Black Belt To Master

Achieving Black Belt is a great achievement. Literally, for martial artists, and metaphorically, for people who have developed the qualities that we have covered so far.

But in traditional martial arts, Black Belt is the BEGINNING of the journey. Achieving Black Belt has been likened to learning the letters of the alphabet. Now it is time to start making words, sentences, paragraphs... even a whole book.

We will now look at nine advanced Black Belt techniques and strategies that take us beyond Black Belt, that take us to mastery.

As masters, we teach, motivate and inspire others to become Black Belts. And THEY go on to become the masters of tomorrow.

I Focus

"I fear not the man who has practiced 10,000 kicks once,
but I fear the man who has practised one kick 10,000 times."
Bruce Lee

When we focus on one thing, we can achieve true mastery. Top chess masters focus on one square. The square they want to control, that they believe is crucial to the next few moves, the next part of the game. Total focus on one square out of the 64 squares on a chessboard.

FOCUS can be represented by:

Follow
One
Course
Until
Successful

In a karate class, if a child is looking uncoordinated or not as sharp as the others, I ask them to focus on something in front of them. It might just be a mark on a distant wall. And then I hold their head still as they move forwards performing the technique.
This gives them more focus. The technique ALWAYS improves.
When we do techniques with focus, we have meaning and power.
Focusing gives us more power.

Avoid negatives
You get what you focus on. And our brains are hard-wired to be alert to dangers and threats. This is part of our basic programming, part of the natural 'fight or flight' response.
We have to see the tiger before the tiger eats us!
In our modern lives, we very rarely have to confront a tiger. But there are two specific problems that we can have:

1 We focus on fear. And the more we focus on fear the more afraid we become.

Three common fears are fear of death, fear of being alone or of dying alone, and fear of financial insecurity. When I have spoken at speaking events about 95% of the audience have at least one of these three fears! So if someone works in the media and is trying to connect with people, people who read their news stories, they focus on one or more of these three fears. They cover areas such as economic uncertainty, falling house prices, terrorism, negative aspects of growing old and so on.

People connect with this, because it taps in to our deepest fears. So more newspapers are sold, more tweets are read and shared, more websites get more views. Black Belt Masters limit their exposure to negativity and fear.

2 We focus on scarcity, rather than abundance. And as Romilla Ready, co-author of *NLP for Dummies* points out, in our thoughts, in the universal consciousness, we can have an abundance. An abundance of scarcity!

To overcome this, we can use some of the concepts we have covered previously:

Do some *Mokuso* (Awareness 4 *Mokuso*)

Model a top positive-focused person (Strategy 6 Modelling)

Change your negative self-talk (Spirit 5 self-talk)

Focus on positive things like your strengths (Spirit 6 Strengths)

More than one problem?

Imagine you have two attackers. You can't fight them both at the same time, unless by some miracle they are both within the exact same range simultaneously.

Military strategy says that where there are two problems, two attackers, tackle the smaller weaker one first.

So how do Black Belt Masters deal with more than one problem? One at a time, starting with the smaller one first.

World Champion

> My *sensei*, Malcolm Phipps, once saw Mie Nakayama, the Ladies *Kata* World Champion practising before she was about to compete in a tournament.

> The *kata* was about 45 moves long. She practised one move, then the same move again, then the same move again, then the same move again. She practised the one move about 50 times.

This is the focus of a world champion. Being totally focused on one thing, doing it until it feels right, until we know it is right. This is what world champions do.

Black Belt Masters take one thing, one problem, one idea, one thought, one move to practise, and they are totally focused on that one thing. This is the Power Of One.

One Thing You Can DO Now:

Working on a specific piece of work on your PC? Close down all other applications. Close your browser, your Facebook, your email. Focus. Focus on the one thing you want to work on, either for a set amount of time (perhaps at first just for 5 or 10 minutes) or until you have progressed to a certain point.

2 Leaders

Black Belt Masters are leaders. They motivate, they inspire, they teach. And they progress themselves.

Journey

The word '*sensei*' means not teacher, but one who has gone before. Someone who has already travelled the path that their 'students' are currently on. Someone who can pass on to others what they have learned for themselves, so far. It is by teaching others that we appreciate what we already know, and continue to learn ourselves. Teaching others helps us to progress to the next level.

And because the people who will 'follow' you know you are on a journey, they will automatically have alignment with you, and you with them. They have an understanding of where you are going, and they are heading in the same direction.

In life, in business, when we have alignment we generate amazing results. We have shared goals, similar values, and we have the discipline and commitment to make things happen. We are a powerful team, who can learn much from each other.

Who can be a Black Belt and a leader?

Who are the people who go on to become Black Belts and then masters? The answer is anyone. ANYONE can be a Black Belt.

> A blind girl passed her 1st Dan grading exam; for the fighting, she fought with her instructor, who was blindfolded.
> People in wheelchairs become Black Belts. Dirk Robertson has been awarded the OBE for his services to teaching physically handicapped children in the UK.

Who can be a Black Belt? You can.
Who can become a master? You can.

Inspire

Masters don't just lead and manage. They inspire. They get the top performance out of their 'followers', not because their followers have been told to do it, but because they want to.

And when masters do something they commit 100%, with the total intent of seeing it through.

Great leaders inspire others to follow them.

Great leaders make a difference.

Praise

Praise is positive reinforcement where good performance and progress are noticed.

Many adults can go weeks, months or even years without receiving any praise.

Occasionally, just occasionally, my instructor will say "That's good, Nick". I am 54 years old, I have been doing karate for 28 years, I am not a child, but those three words get me from being motivated to super motivated.

Sometimes when I praise a child in my karate class, for having practised, for having improved a particular technique, I ask them when was the last time that someone said they had done well.

Sometimes the answer is "never".What I have noticed over the years is that when I praise a child for something, they try harder, they do more practising at home.

Praise, given sincerely, has real power. Power to inspire.

Leaders praise others. Leaders find excuses to give praise, they PLAN to give praise (such as sending Thank You cards). And they know that the most powerful, sincere type of praise is spontaneous. So they use their *zanshin* to be constantly alert for situations where they can immediately give praise.

Praise: Positive
                Remarks that
                Actively
                Inspire
                Someone
                Else

You do, they do

Having the power of a leader is big responsibility. Other people will follow your actions.

> Daniel Rabson is a distributor with Utility Warehouse, a UK telecoms and utilities company. They operate on an MLM (multi-level marketing) basis.
>
> Daniel has over 900 distributors in his personal network, some of whom are direct, and some who are distributors of his distributors, and so on.
>
> It is a network that he has built up over many years. Daniel has noticed one key thing about his direct distributors, the people one level down in his 'down line':
>
> "They do what you do."
>
> So when he stops recruiting new people into his own network, his direct distributors do the same. When he starts recruiting, so do they. People follow people. His direct distributors have their own network, with their own direct distributors. So when THEY start recruiting, so do THEIR direct distributors. And this 'ripple' effect continues down the chain.
>
> Daniel's actions have a massive cascade effect, affecting up to 900 people.

When you are a leader, other people will do what you do.

Whether they are consciously modelling you (Strategy 6 Modelling) because they want to have the success that you are having, or unconsciously. In either situation, they will do what you do.

Black Belt Masters are aware of how much they influence others. They give praise whenever they can, and they lead by example, in everything they do.

One Thing You Can DO Now:

Right now, find a reason to give someone some praise. The 'someone' could be a child, a parent, a partner, work colleague,

customer, supplier, a friend. Find a reason to give them praise and go and do it now. Do it with integrity and do not expect anything in return.

3 Yame

Yame means stop.

With a beginner on their first lesson, who is really keen to START, I tell them how to STOP.

I tell them that if something hurts, they must stop. If something hurts, it is not right. It might be my fault, maybe I did not explain a technique properly. When beginners are about to start some gentle fighting for the first time, I remind them about *Yame*.

They have to know that when I shout "*Yame*", they are to stop. Maybe I have seen something that is about to happen in their 'fight'. Maybe something has happened with other people, and I have to stop the class. Maybe it is time for them to partner up with someone different, or because we are about to move on to the next part of the lesson.

But *Yame* also has more advanced implications.

Too many people, in life and in business, carry on with something when they should just stop. Perhaps it is their ego getting in the way of making a rational decision. Perhaps they are too caught up in what they are doing and have lost the ability to see the bigger picture.

Yame and prospects

In business, too much sales effort can be focused on prospects that it seems we just can't close. This wastes our time, our money and our energy. Having a long list of prospects that we just can't seem to close also lulls us in to a false sense of security. We look at our sales pipeline and think that the next two or three months will be great, because some of these long-standing prospects will surely close that month. Won't they?

We have to know when to call it a day, to force the *Yame*. To stop wasting time with that prospect, perhaps by walking away or giving them an ultimatum or a genuine once-in-a-lifetime offer. This will free up our time, money and energy to focus on other prospects, some of whom WILL close soon, and develop new prospects.

Top sales performers, the masters of sales, know when to call it a day and move on. This helps them keep motivated, as they are always predominantly focused on prospects who will close, so their conversion rate is high and stays high.

Yame and selling

When selling to a prospect, or selling something to an existing customer, when you reach agreement and they say Yes, STOP.

When you have got agreement, stop. Job done. It is over. It's finished. Mission accomplished.

Yame and business

One of the first questions that business coaches ask a new client is about their exit plan. Do they have one, and if so when do they plan to exit?

In other words, how do they plan to STOP?

Have you got an exit plan?

Black Belt Masters know when to stop. They put any ego to one side, and make a rational decision where they cut any losses and live to fight another day.

One Thing You Can DO Now:

Got something that has been dragging on? Something that you are honestly fed up with? What would happen if you just stopped? If you just walked away?

4 Difficult

Black Belt Masters know that the road they have travelled has at times been a difficult one. And that there will be new difficulties ahead.

It is meant to be

A few years ago a complete beginner turned up for her first karate lesson. She was about 25, and had never trained in a martial art before.
She was brilliant! Everything seemed to come naturally. The stances, the focus, the timing, the co-ordination. The flexibility to kick high. Everything was almost perfect. In time she was going to be an awesome Black Belt.
She never trained again.
It was too easy, for her.

Sometimes, some things in life are just meant to be difficult. Let's say that I promised you that if at the end of ONE karate lesson you could do a few simple techniques, I would award you a Black Belt.
What would you have? You would have a piece of black cotton about 2.5 metres long. And nothing else.
Black Belt Masters know that one of the main reasons they are a Black Belt is because of the difficulties they have overcome. The fights that they have had, not with others, but with themselves.
By overcoming difficulties through our own hard work and persistence, we are training ourselves to be successful. To learn how we get through the dark challenging times, learning about the strategies that work for us, fully understanding our own resources that we have available to us.
And then, when things go wrong, we just work harder.

"The drop of water wears the stone hollow
not by force but by persistence."
Bruce Lee

Studies show that people who are more positive, more hopeful and more optimistic, are those who believe in hard work and persistence. When things go wrong, they don't worry or feel hopeless, they just work harder and smarter.

Easy or difficult

When I find my karate 'easy', the advice I have been given by my instructors is to train harder.

When I find my karate difficult, the advice I have been given by my instructors is to train harder.

Acceptance

Chantal Cornelius is a Marketing Consultant with over 20 years' experience of helping companies to grow their businesses. She is a keen runner, but lives in a dip, surrounded by hills.

So when she goes running, the first part of her run is always uphill. She was doing all the hard work at the start of her run, and this was affecting the extent to which she enjoyed the whole run. As Chantal says, "If the 'you can't do this' voice gets a hold early on, I find it harder to get rid of it and it keeps coming back throughout the run."

We discussed several ideas about how she could address this mentally. We discussed the benefits of getting up early in the run on to the top of a hill, so that she could enjoy the scenery. About how she could use the first part of the run as a final warm-up exercise.

A few months after the conversation I asked her what, if anything, had made a difference. The one thing that had made a difference was that she accepted that the first part of the run was the most difficult. She just accepted it. This also helped her have a more positive attitude, and she now views the uphill start of the run as helping her to get even fitter and cope better with other hills when she goes running on other routes.

"Accepting that I have to start uphill reminds me to shut the voice up and then I can get on and enjoy my run."

Difficult can be good

Assuming that you have a job or a business, assume just for a few moments that your line of work is actually very easy. There have been no difficulties in launching or buying or growing a business. Or, if you are in a job, it was so easy to get those qualifications, and develop a great CV by winning those promotions or moving to better roles with other companies.

Anyone could have done it. Anyone could do what you do for a living. It is easy to be just like you.

What would that look like? What it would look like is that there would be thousands, possibly millions, of people competing with you for your business's customers or for your job. You would get paid less. In fact, there would be so much supply that you probably wouldn't have a job or a business.

You'd have no income. You'd be miserable. Your partner might leave you. You would lose your house because you wouldn't be able to pay the mortgage or the rent. So now you're unemployed, single, homeless, and probably pretty miserable.

Now stop those negative thoughts!

Difficult can be good.

The next time you find something difficult in your life, whether in business or in your personal life, focus on the positives. It is these difficulties that pay you money, that make you special, that give you some of the things in life that are worth having.

Black Belt Masters don't just accept that sometimes in life things are difficult. They actively welcome difficult situations, because they know that these are great opportunities for us to get better, to improve and develop our skills, to empower ourselves to create our future success.

One Thing You Can DO Now:

Think of something you are struggling with, something that you are finding difficult. Why is this difficulty a good thing? What skills will you learn when overcoming this challenge? What will you learn about yourself that will be helpful to you in the future?

5 PMA *(Positive Mental Attitude)*

Black Belt Masters have a positive mental attitude, and know how to keep it, even when things are going against them.

> Paul Herbert was a top karate fighter, competing in karate tournaments all over the world. Sometimes in a fight he would get hit first, so his opponent would be ahead on points scored.
>
> Paul would then think that HE had just scored the point. So all he had to do was to resume the fight, and do what he had 'already done'. Even though what he had 'already done' was only in his mind.
>
> Even though he had just suffered a negative experience (going a point down), mentally he was positive, he was ahead. This positive mental attitude helped him win fights when he had gone a point down and was losing.

Every time you experience a 'bad' event (except maybe really traumatic ones), think of one positive aspect that you can take from the experience. Something you can learn, something you can take away that will be of use to you in the future.

Get some scars

Black Belt Masters have a positive attitude about getting scars.

When we get scars we are learning a bit about what does work, but a lot about what doesn't! Getting scars is where we have the best opportunity to learn from our mistakes, and from others who are better than us.

It is the Black Belts who are still in the ring, still training and practising, who have most of the scars. The people who have given up, who couldn't take the heat, have gone. They are no longer getting any scars, but they are not training either. They are not progressing.

Keep getting scars. Keep getting better.

Universal Law of Sales

The Universal Law of Sales has helped me win big clients and get big orders. It works time and time again, across many different types of industries, many different types of companies. It works with me, it works with other people.

The Universal Law of Sales says that when you are working on building your business, getting more customers, that as long as you keep focused, with integrity, working intelligently and hard, something positive will happen. It may not be what you think will happen. It may not be directly connected with the activities you have been doing, but something positive will happen. It will be an unexpected order. It will be a prospect you last spoke to six months ago who said "No", who contacts you out of the blue and says "Yes, let's go ahead now."

You must be focused and working intelligently. So if, for example, you are spending time and energy in making cold calls, or doing social media, and you have been working on this for a good while, it is probably time to focus your efforts on something else.

Visualisation

When I went for my third Dan Black Belt grading, I was a bit fed up with failing the exam the first time, then retaking it and passing as had happened with both my first and my second Dan gradings. This was nobody's fault but my own.

I wanted to pass my third Dan the first time. There were two things I did differently in my preparation for the exam. They were both to do with visualisation.

I visualised performing every single part of the exam, every technique, perfectly. I visualised this happening in different parts of the hall where the grading exam was to be held. I visualised me walking to my allotted area from the right hand side of the hall. And from the left hand side.

The other thing I did was to have some hypnotherapy to help overcome the effects of having been bullied at school. This was 30 years ago, but I knew there were issues to be addressed. I visualised that by achieving my third Dan, I would be casting these demons aside. I visualised that as it was announced that I had reached the standard required, I would be free of the negative thoughts and emotions that had been with me for 30 years.

I passed first time.

Black Belt Masters visualise positivity in everything they do. If you look for negatives, if you focus on negatives, you will find them. If you focus on positives, you will find THEM!

> "As you think, so shall you become."
> Bruce Lee

If you focus on the problem, you will continue to have a problem. If you focus on the solution, you will find the solution. Visualise the problem being resolved, visualise the solution happening. And visualise how that makes you feel.

Patience

Black Belt Masters know that some things take longer than we would like. But they remain positive, because they have patience. They know the good things in life are worth waiting for.

A key experiment that showed the value of patience was the Stanford Marshmallow experiment, which focused on delayed gratification.

In the experiment in 1960, children were told they could have a marshmallow now, but that if they waited for 15 minutes they could have two marshmallows! One third of the children waited the full 15 minutes before eating two marshmallows. Subsequent studies done over the next 40 years showed that these children went on to achieve more academically, be healthier, less stressed, and generally fared better in life.

The karate grading system teaches patience. The first seven gradings are done every three months. The next three gradings, culminating in the grading for the first Black Belt, are six months apart. So to get to Black Belt takes almost four years.

Then to get to second Dan takes a minimum of 2 years. Then to get to third Dan takes a minimum of 3 years. And so on.

By the time we get to say, sixth Dan, we have been doing karate for a minimum of 24 years!

Black Belt Masters know the power of patience. The good things in life take time. They are worth waiting for and they are worth fighting for.

Black Belt Masters reject rejection. They will fall down seven times and they will get up eight. Black Belt Masters have a positive mental attitude.

One Thing You Can DO Now:

Think of something bad that you might have experienced recently. What is one positive thing that you can take away from the experience, that you can use to your advantage next time?

6 Before

Black Belt Masters know that there are three parts to any one event, to any one activity.

There is what happens BEFORE the event.
There is the actual moment of the event.
And there is what happens AFTER the event, the follow through.

It is too easy to focus on the actual moment. But what usually determines if the 'moment' is an effective or happy one, is what has happened before, and what will happen afterwards.

"My oh my"

Black Belt Masters know that one of their best weapons that they will use for fighting is their concept of *maai* ('my'). *Maai* means distance or interval. It is the countdown of what happens BEFORE the event. As we get nearer to the actual event happening, the *maai* will shorten.

When dealing with problems, the first question to ask is "Is the problem a problem?" Sometimes the distance (*maai*) between us and the problem is so great that there is no point in worrying about it.

Imagine I have a knife and want to attack you (make sure you imagine this, because honestly I don't!). Well, I live in Reading in the UK which is where I probably am right now, and the chances are you aren't. At the moment you are quite safe from my knife attack! It is just not a problem, at the moment.

 If you think you have a problem, before worrying about it, make sure it IS a problem. Is it something that is going to affect you any time soon? If not, it is not a problem, the distance is too big, so don't worry about it.

The problem only becomes a problem when the *maai* becomes much shorter.

Maai in sales

In sales, the concept of *maai* can be used to understand the sales cycle. The sales cycle is the process a prospect goes through before actually buying the product or service. It is different with every product and service. Even with the same product or service, the sales cycle can be slightly different for different people.

Let's say a prospect needs to go through six or seven steps before they decide to buy. A 'step' could be an enquiry they make from a website, sending them an email with some information, then speaking with them, having a meeting, them getting approval from other people, making sure the finance is in place to pay, then getting the order raised.

Of course the process will vary across different industries and different markets and different target customers. But one principle will hold true; you can't massively jump the *maai*.

You won't go from sending someone an email to getting an order from them if they need to get approval from other people first, and make sure the finance is in place.

Black Belt Masters know that at each stage in the sales cycle, what they are selling is to get to the next step! They know that you can't go from White Belt immediately to Black Belt, it is just impossible. This applies to getting an order, to getting a job, to getting someone (hopefully) to love you.

Understanding their *maai*, their buying process, will mean that you can work with them, and possibly help them with some of the steps.

For example, you could have a paper ready on why buying this product makes sense financially, for the prospect to give to their financial decision maker. A paper that is written in language that financial people identify with.

Maai in networking

In networking, the concept of *maai* explains why some people get networking so wrong. Because they have met someone at a networking event and are talking to a real person, a real living breathing human being, they think they are at an advanced stage in the sales cycle. (Face-to-face meetings usually happen several steps into the process, when there is genuine interest and the prospect is showing some commitment, usually in terms of the time they have already spent on considering your services.) So they think they are close to the 'moment' when the deal is done and the order is raised. So they sell!

But the person they are speaking to is not even thinking about buying, or introducing them to a contact of theirs, or isn't even the right person.

Although face-to-face, because we are networking we are actually only at the beginning of the sales cycle. There is very little trust in the relationship at such an early stage. The next step, the event to focus on, is to get their agreement to send them an email. Or perhaps to connect on LinkedIn, or to have a meeting and a chat over a cup of coffee. Trust and credibility have to be established before there can be a meaningful face-to-face meeting.

Black Belt Masters in business know the maai of the sales cycle. They 'sell' the prospect just the next step in the process, they keep shortening the maai, until the deal is done or the introduction is made to a useful contact.

One Thing You Can DO Now:

Think of something you want, something that is big. What is the NEXT step you need to focus on in order to make it happen? Focus on this, and make this happen, and you will have shortened the maai to your target.

7 Follow through

I do some demonstrations with a break-board where I explain that I am going to hit the board very hard. I say that every time I have hit the board it has broken. I am going to hit it with everything I have got.

But this time the board will not break. Why?

Because I will not follow through. With a good awareness of distance, my knuckles will touch the board, with full force, but will not follow through. They will either stay where they are, just touching the board, or pull back slightly.

It is only what happens AFTER I hit the board that makes the board break. If there is no follow through, there is no break. It is only what has happened afterwards that has made the 'event' worthwhile, that has meant the event has been successful.

Any follow through will do

SOMETHING must happen after the event, there must be a follow through. After you have met someone interesting at a networking event, won a big sale, asked someone out on a date.

It does not matter what the follow through is, it just has to be something. In karate one of the first techniques we teach beginners is a front snap kick. The knee is raised, then the lower leg extended to make the kick, AND THEN the leg is snapped back. The foot is then put on the floor.

It is the snapping back of the leg that gives the kick its power[1].

[1]You might be thinking why does hitting the board and then possibly pulling back mean the technique has no power, but doing a front snap kick and then pulling back means the kick is effective? It is because of maai (distance). When the board is hit, the knuckles just touch the board. The contact that is made can vary by the thickness of the skin covering the knuckles, which at most is about 1 millimetre. When the kick is performed, if it was to be performed in real life, in a self-defence situation, there would be full contact between the foot and the attacker, to the extent that the attacker would feel the force of the kick. Some of their body would move as it absorbed the impact. Snapping back the foot then adds extra energy to the technique.

This is the same principle that you may have experienced in flicking a towel. If you put one end of a towel in your hand, when you extend the arm fast, and keep it extended, the towel follows, and then drops to the floor. But if you extend the arm fast and immediately snap it back, the towel goes out and then flies back towards you. And you hear a snap, indicating there is a lot of energy being generated.

Even though the follow 'through' is away from the actual event, away from the impact area, it is the follow through that gives the event real power.

The best exponent of the AFTERS concept is Andy Bounds, who in his book *The Jelly Effect* describes how to use the AFTERS concept in our communication. *The Jelly Effect* is one of the few books that I have read more than once.

The success of everything we do, whether it is fighting, communicating, doing business or falling in love, is based on the afters, the follow through. There is no point in sending a man to the moon if you can't get him back.

Hit rate

We can use the concept of 'follow through' to meaningfully evaluate whether an 'event' has been successful. It is often not about the event itself, but what happened after the event. Whether the event is a punch, or a business meeting (hopefully not both at the same time!), or an email you have sent.

Follow through means we are talking about results. Whether an event was successful. Or not.

Now we are talking in this language, we can now be even more meaningful and talk about how often? How often is this event successful in the follow through? What is the hit rate of this event in terms of delivering the desired follow through?

In life you will meet many people who will tell you of amazing successes they have played a part in. But what was their hit rate?

This applies in business, in life. What if I told you I know a doctor who had saved a terminally ill patient from dying? That's a WOW! That is impressive. But what if I knew that the other 9,999 terminally ill patients they had treated had all died. That's not so impressive.

When someone is telling you something, something that they have a vested interest in, think of the hit rate. If there has been one 'success', how many failures have there been?

Black Belt Masters always follow through, with everything they do, and cut through the hype by looking at the hit rate, to know if something is really successful.

One Thing You Can DO Now:

Think of one follow through you can do now with something that you thought had finished, and do it.

8 Shuhari (the journey to mastery)

The journey to becoming a Black Belt Master can be described by the Japanese word *shuhari*. It is pronounced shoe-hah-ree.
Shuhari is actually three separate words:

Shu is the Japanese word for obedience. It refers to learning by obedience or mechanical repetition. At this first stage we are learning by faithfully following the existing teachings and practices. At the *shu* stage the emphasis is on constant learning.
Shu is about learning technique rather than understanding. A beginner at their first karate lesson is at the '*shu*' stage, and will be until they get to Black Belt.

Ha is the Japanese word for divergence. It refers to coming to an understanding by constant practice, an understanding of the art, and an understanding of ourselves. We have reached the level of *mushin* (Spirit 9 Practising), where everything seems automatic, where we operate with 'no mind'. We have reached unconscious competence.
This is the stage where we start to break with tradition, where we start to try new concepts and ideas. At '*ha*' we are asking questions of what we have learned so far.

Ri is the Japanese word for transcendence. It is where we achieve mastery. We are creating our own journey, going where no-one has travelled before. The student has become the master.
This is where there is a high level of creativity, where we take the art to the next level.
Shuhari therefore means to initially learn from tradition, then break the chains of tradition and finally transcend tradition (from *The Little Book of Seishinkai*).
It means to start by closely following the way, and then ultimately coming up with 'our' way.

Ri and leadership
At *Ri*, at transcendence, our creativity is high. We are pioneers, developing

new techniques, new strategies, new concepts and new ways of thinking. We are leading others consciously and unconsciously, attracting people to us. People who will follow us because they have an idea of the journey we are on and want to be a part of it.

We are leaders, showing others the way, for them to start the process of *shu-ha-ri*.

Being aware of the concept of *shuhari* will help us develop others to become leaders, by helping them to progress to the next stage at the right time. Whether in business, personal life, or perhaps in a sport or hobby, the leaders of today are teaching the leaders of tomorrow, the masters of the future.

Black Belt Masters lead and inspire others to become the masters of the future.

One Thing You Can DO Now:

Think of something that you are really good at, a skill you have. How can you help others achieve this level of expertise? What one thing can you do now that will help someone progress and develop their skill?

9 Your Journey

You have arrived at the end of this book. You are at the end of this particular journey.

You are a Black Belt Master.

You have the awareness of a Black Belt Master. You avoid trouble, and you react fast, meaning you can seize opportunities and make changes quickly. You take responsibility for yourself, and you internalise what is useful to you. You externalise negativity whilst learning from your mistakes. You live in the present and feel connected to what is around you, especially the people who matter in your life. You know who you are, what your values are and how they motivate you to achieve the successes that you have experienced so far. You are aware of what you already know, the life experiences you can use to help yourself and be of service to others. You are aware that you control what you put in to your Circle of Life, and this empowers you to achieve more success. Part of your life's journey is to expand your comfort zone to the point where you always feel comfortable and in control. You are aware of the different roles you have, but you present one face to the world, your true face, because you know and appreciate who you really are. You maintain a high state of awareness to reduce unnecessary risks, so that you are well placed to look after yourself and others, in life and in business. And you are aware of the importance of fun. You know how to switch off, to go and have a good time.

You are a Black Belt Master.

You have the strategy of a Black Belt Master. You understand the importance of the journey of how to get to where you want to be. You are intent on making your own way, going on your journey. This is your life and you are going to live it. You break down your goals and your challenges into parts, and you have a system for how you will do each part. You know that you control your systems. You understand the importance of other people's strategies, in life, in business and in love. You have the confidence to ask them what their strategies are. You take strategies from one area of your life and you apply them to other areas, meaning you can replicate success across different journeys in different areas of your life. You model top performers so that you achieve more. You know how to build rapport and trust with people, and you know the importance of the 'why', yours and theirs. You are comfortable handling objections. You understand what culture is and why it is important, and you recognise a culture by observing patterns of behaviour.

You are a Black Belt Master.

You have the spirit of a Black Belt Master. You will never fail at anything, because you will never give up. You know you will make mistakes, and that this is OK. You know you will always fight on, especially when you are down. You are aware of the power of your beliefs, and you know that beliefs, especially limiting beliefs, are not reality. You know that any limiting beliefs reveal themselves in the *ninjas* of negative self-talk. And you know how to defeat these *ninjas*. You know what your strengths are, and you play to them, ignoring your weaknesses. You continually work to develop your strengths. You know that setbacks, however significant they appear at the time, are just a part of the journey. You ask questions, of yourself and of others, so that you and they can get what you both want. You put in the extra effort, the extra practice, to make sure you get the things that are worth having. You are self-aware and you know your cause is just. This awareness gives you confidence and courage, and you accept the consequences of your actions.

You are a Black Belt Master.

You have the humility of a Black Belt Master. You know that humility has real power, the power to deliver lasting change. You maintain humility by playing down your ego and you avoid posturing. At times you can be happy to give way, to concede something that you might want, to make a particular journey that little bit easier for someone else. You value your high self-esteem and you have a high self-worth. You know how to maintain your high self-esteem. You take the long-term view, so you can maintain your cool in a crisis. You are assertive, never aggressive, always looking at the bigger picture. You have an attitude of gratitude and you practise gratitude whenever you can. You care and think about other people. You don't judge others because you know we are all different, we all have our strengths and weaknesses. You feel you are a part of something bigger than yourself, which keeps short-term obstacles and setbacks in perspective. You choose the simplicity of humility over the complication that arises from ego.

You are a Black Belt Master.

You make decisions like a Black Belt Master. You never wait for the perfect time, because you know it does not exist. You never aim for perfection, because perfection is too fluid a concept, and one person's perfection is another person's imperfection. Instead you adopt the principle of *kaizen*, making small improvements, step by step, one thing at a time. When you do act, you act with certainty and confidence, free of doubt. You are aware of and understand the three ways in which we can move forwards; you act decisively with full commitment, or you prepare first and then make your move, or you go and get it quickly. You keep yourself motivated intrinsically, and you know whether you are a 'go to' person or an 'away from' person. You have high self-discipline, so when you have made a decision you go and take action and you follow it through. You know the importance of trust. You trust yourself, and you trust others, given time. You understand that totally committing to something has a power all of its own. You just do things; you know that doing nothing is usually the worst option.

You are a Black Belt Master.

You have the focus of a Black Belt Master because you focus on one positive thing at a time. You lead like a Black Belt Master because you inspire others to do what you do and you find excuses to give praise. You know when to stop, so that you don't over commit or waste time unnecessarily. You accept that at times some things will be difficult, and at these times you focus on the positives. You know you will get scars and that these will help you improve. You visualise positive outcomes and you are patient, because sometimes the good things take that little bit longer. You know that with everything that happens in your life there is a before and an after. You only deal with problems if they are a problem, and you understand the process people go through before they commit. You know that so much depends on what happens after the actual event, on the follow through. You understand the process by which you become a master, and this enables you to guide and inspire the Black Belt Masters of tomorrow.

You are a Black Belt Master.

You are in control of yourself and your destiny.

You control your journey.

The rest of your journey starts now.

Go well.

"If you always put limits on what you can do, physical or anything else, it'll spread over into the rest of your life. It'll spread into your work, into your morality, into your entire being. There are no limits. There are plateaus, but you must not stay there, you must go beyond them."
Bruce Lee

Bibliography

Andy Bounds	The Jelly Effect
The Success Principles	Jack Canfield
The 7 Habits of Highly Effective People	Stephen Covey
Good To Great	Jim Collins
Power vs Force	David R Hawkins
The Little Book of Seishinkai	Malcolm Phipps (SSKI Handbook)
NLP for Dummies	Romilla Ready and Kate Burton
Delivering Happiness	Tony Hsieh

Acknowledgments

Many people have helped me on my journey so far, and I am grateful to each one of them.

Firstly, thanks to my three karate instructors over the last 28 years. Each in their own way has been an exceptional role model. Chronologically in terms of my training they are:–

Sensei Rod Butler, 6th Dan, SKE (Shotokan Karate England) Chief Instructor. Thank you for lighting the spark that continues 28 years later.

Sensei John van Weenen OBE, 8th Dan, TASK (Traditional Association of Shotokan Karate) Chief Instructor. I am in awe of your humanitarian achievements.

Sensei Malcolm Phipps, 8th Dan, SSKI (Seishinkai Shotokan Karate International) Chief Instructor. You are a teacher, a friend, and you inspire me in more ways than you know. Thank you.

I would also like to mention the late Derek Barnet from TASK, who gained his 3rd Dan at the age of 65 and through his dedication and loyalty taught me so much.

Romilla Ready, who got me started me on this book, many years ago!

Steve Bishop (http://www.stevebishop-hypnotherapy.co.uk/) the hypnotherapist I consulted who played a part in my gaining Third Dan at the first attempt.

The culture of Givers Gain™ in BNI goes to the very top of this remarkable organisation. People I know in and via BNI are Ivan Misner, Frank de Raffele, and Andy Bounds. Thank you.

A massive thank you to Rick Armstrong, Rachel Topping, Samantha Richardson and all the team of Fisher King Publishing, you are amazing!

Other people who have helped me with this book include Christine Wilson, Paul Herbert, Becki Wilson, Keith Mitchell, Rintu Basu, Lynne Greenmoor, Lauren Greenmoor, Julian Lewis, Simon Speed, Daniel Rabson, Mike

Samuels, Ian Wilson, Tony Hoare, George Hoare, Louise Lothian, James Walsh, Barry Tindall, Marc Rocker, Rebecca Jones. Thank you.

Thank you to my friends and colleagues in the PSA (Professional Speaking Association); Tim Luscombe, Peter Green, Dave Hyner, Deri Llewellyn-Davies, Chantal Cornelius, and Jacqui Hogan.

About the Author

Nick Forgham empowers people to achieve more than they think they can. Whether it is improving a martial art technique, or increasing sales, or removing limiting beliefs that are holding them back.

He is a keynote speaker, workshop facilitator and runs retreats and seminars that motivate and inspire people to succeed.

Nick lives in Reading, UK and works internationally.

For more information visit www.nickforgham.com

Think I can help you? Email nick@nickforgham.com

Glossary

Aikido	Japanese martial art, founded by Morihei Ueshiba
Ashi	Foot / leg
BNI	Business Networking International
Budo	The martial way
Bunkai	To break down, often used in relation to the meaning behind a particular technique
Dojo	The place of the way
Dojo Kun	Training hall rules
Judo	Gentle way
Karate	Empty hands
Kata	Form, a pattern of movements
Locus of Control	The extent to which we internalise and take responsibility
Maai	Distance or interval
Mokuso	Time out (literally, clear one's mind)
Oi Ashi	To step forwards
Samurai	Warrior
Seishinkai	Association of mind, spirit and soul
Sensei	Teacher (literally, one who has gone before)
Shuhari	Transcendence
SSKI	Seishinkai Shotokan Karate International
Suri Ashi	To half step forwards
Ushiro Geri	Back Geri
Yame	Stop
Yori Ashi	To slide step forwards
Zanshin	Awareness

Index

A

Active listening 45
Adversity 54
Ageing 59
aggressive 89, 95, 96, 156
Aikido 54, 167
Albert Einstein 84
alignment 19, 51, 76, 134
Andy Bounds 151, 161, 163
anxiety 7
Apple 104
Art of Peace 54
Ashi 116
assertive 8, 89, 95, 96, 156
autonomic nervous system 9
awareness 1, 3, 4, 6, 9, 10, 13, 15, 20, 25, 38, 45, 51, 68, 76, 89, 150, 155, 156

B

Barack Obama 128
Barry Manilow 99
Beijing 79
Beliefs 1, 59, 60, 61, 62, 110
Berkshire 91
Black Belt 1, 2, 2, 3, 4, 7, 8, 9, 1, 2, 3, 5, 6, 14, 15, 18, 23, 25, 30, 32, 33, 38, 53, 54, 56, 58, 64, 69, 73, 76, 78, 84, 101, 106, 111, 118, 119, 123, 129, 130, 132, 133, 134, 136, 139, 140, 142, 143, 144, 145, 146, 147, 148, 149, 152, 153, 154, 155, 156, 157, 158
BNI 1, 2, 54, 65, 91, 92, 114, 124, 163, 167
breathing 9, 29, 33, 112, 148
Bruce Lee 16, 57, 88, 128, 131, 140, 145, 159
Budo 26, 167
Bunkai 7, 26, 45, 46, 167
buyer's remorse 1

C

D

E

F

Feldenkrais, Moshe 33
focus 3, 4, 9, 10, 20, 26, 27, 29, 32, 33, 34, 52, 61, 89, 90, 93, 94, 95, 98, 101,
     105, 110, 112, 113, 115, 120, 131, 132, 133, 138, 140, 142, 144, 145,
     147, 149, 157
Formula One 41

G

Gichin Funakoshi 4, 6, 34, 51, 56, 73, 76, 79, 104
goals 7, 10, 28, 29, 33, 34, 40, 52, 73, 80, 134, 155
Good To Great 80, 161
Google 80
Go with 43
grading 5, 33, 38, 55, 101, 134, 144, 145
gratitude 8, 91, 92, 93, 157
guilt 7

H

Harry Potter 5, 33, 38, 119
Herzberg 119
Hierarchy of Needs 119
Hirokazu Kanazawa 55
homeless 80, 91, 92, 142
Hubble Telescope 109
Humiliation 80, 81
humility 8, 34, 79, 80, 81, 82, 83, 84, 86, 88, 89, 90, 91, 93, 96, 98, 99, 101,
     104, 106, 109, 119, 156, 157

I

internalising 6
intrinsic 118, 119, 120
Introspection 8, 76
Ivan Misner 2, 54, 92, 163

J

Jack Canfield 4, 161
Jim Collins 80, 161
JKA (Japan Karate Association) 101
Jose Mujica 80, 91, 101

Judo 26, 167

K

Kaizen 9, 112
Kara 8, 4, 65, 79
karate 2, 3, 4, 5, 6, 7, 12, 14, 19, 23, 26, 27, 32, 34, 38, 39, 41, 44, 51, 54, 55,
    57, 58, 61, 64, 67, 69, 73, 79, 80, 81, 84, 86, 101, 105, 107, 109, 110,
    112, 116, 118, 121, 123, 125, 131, 135, 140, 141, 143, 145, 150, 153,
    163
kata 14, 24, 39, 45, 55, 133
knife attacks 21, 104

L

Lancaster 93
Lao-Tzu 4, 10, 84
Limiting Beliefs 61, 110
LinkedIn 30, 124, 149
Little Book of Seishinkai 23, 98, 153, 161
Locus of Control 5, 16, 17, 118, 167
Los Angeles 14, 67
losing weight 39

M

maai 147, 148, 149
Mahatma Gandhi 80
Malcolm Phipps 19, 24, 67, 83, 101, 133, 161, 163
Marathon des Sables 82
Martin Luther King 5, 88
Maslow 119
mastery 4, 130, 131, 153
Mie Nakayama 133
Mindfulness 7
mistakes 2, 17, 55, 87, 127, 143, 155, 156
Miyamoto Musashi 35, 48, 86
Modelling 7, 41, 42, 132, 136
Mokuso 7, 9, 10, 11, 13, 19, 132, 167
Morihei Ueshiba 54, 70, 167
Mother Teresa 98
Motivation 9, 12, 118, 119

Motorola 30
Muhammad Ali 54, 58, 69, 73

N

negative self-talk 8, 64, 65, 66, 123, 132, 156
Nelson Mandela 76, 80, 89, 101
networking 4, 16, 91, 92, 93, 94, 102, 103, 124, 148, 150
NHS (National Health Service) 93
ninja 65, 66, 93, 94
NLP 132, 161
nocebo 59

O

Oi Ashi 116, 117, 167

P

pain 9, 33, 62, 63, 119
Patience 145
patterns 7, 14, 51, 52, 156
Paul Herbert 143, 163
Pierre Omidyar 70
Placebo 59
PMA (Positive Mental Attitude) 143
practising 8, 38, 73, 74, 75, 92, 133, 135, 143

R

rapport 43, 44, 46, 49, 72, 156
Reading 91, 147, 165
Red Belt 33
Regret 8, 60
rejection 146
responsibility 4, 5, 6, 16, 17, 18, 65, 118, 136, 155, 167
revising 30
risk 7, 21, 22, 123
Robben Island 89, 101
Robert Zajonc 124
Romilla Ready 132, 161, 163

S

T

U

Utility Warehouse 136

V

values 4, 12, 13, 19, 51, 76, 77, 101, 134, 155
Visualisation 144

W

White Belt 33, 148
Winston Churchill 70

Y

Yame 9, 121, 138, 139, 167
Yoda 126
Yori Ashi 117, 167

Z

Zanshin 7, 1, 13, 19, 167
Zappos 80
zen 112

"Who wouldn't want to be a Business Ninja? This book gives you the mindset, tools and techniques to do so. You'll discover simple ways to achieve more, in less time, and enjoy the ride. A revelation."

Andy Bounds
Best-selling author, award-winning consultant and creator of
www.andyboundsonline.com

"I am thrilled Nick took up my suggestion to share his knowledge and wisdom. It was obvious to me that, as a black belt and businessman, Nick could offer people a winning formula for success in both their business and their personal lives. Reading just one of the 'secrets' first thing in the morning makes for an ideal start and a great way to set the intention for creating your perfect day."

Romilla Ready
Co-author 'NLP for Dummies'

"A truly excellent work bringing the world of karate and the world of business together in an exciting and easy to understand format."

Malcolm Phipps
8th Dan, SSKI Chief Instructor

"This book gives you sage advice on how to improve yourself personally and professionally so that you are more able to achieve your MASSIVE goals. Much of the great content is backed up by my research into top achievers over eighteen years, so take heed, take action, read this book!"

David Hyner
Researcher, author and professional speaker

Lightning Source UK Ltd.
Milton Keynes UK
UKOW06f0334010616

275374UK00011B/55/P